A Complete Guide

picture
framing
a complete guide

ARMAND FOSTER

A & C Black • London

Acknowledgements

I'd like to express my sincere thanks to Malcolm Clarke in Scunthorpe for his patient help in producing the sequential photographs and to Penny Scott (Managing Director) of Euromouldings and her staff, Rob Lelliott, Kevin Shaw and Anna Puglia for their general help. Finally my wife Cheryl for all her help.

First published in Great Britain in 2006
A & C Black Publishers Limited
38 Soho Square
London W1D 3HB
www.acblack.com

ISBN-10: 0-7136-7386-9
ISBN-13: 978-0-7136-7386-9
Copyright © 2006 Armand Foster

CIP Catalogue records for this book are available from the British Library and the U.S. Library of Congress.

Armand Foster has asserted his right under the Copyright, Design and Patents Act, 1988, to be identified as the author of this work.

Book design by Paula McCann
Cover design by Sutchinda Rangsi Thompson
Copyedited by Julian Beecroft
Managing Editor: Susan Kelly
Image origination: Armand Foster

Printed and bound in China by C&C Offset Printing Co.Ltd.

A & C Black uses paper produced with elemental chlorine-free pulp, harvested from managed sustainable forests.

CONTENTS

PREFACE

This book is designed to be a complete guide to picture framing. It endeavours to include all the information that could ever be required, in as simple a format as possible, to help guide you through the process of framing a picture at whatever standard you want to achieve, from framing a couple of pictures on the kitchen table to running a fully fledged business.

Once you have started, you will find framing addictive, interesting, rewarding and satisfying. But you will also need to be careful, self-critical and patient. Like anything worthwhile, it takes practise, whether you are working on the kitchen table or in a fully established workshop. Remember to get it right! Once you have finished the frame, you or someone else will have to live with the result. A crooked mount, scratched glass, bad mitres: all will return to haunt you.

Practise and be critical of your work, and do not let faults pass you by: it is far better to recut a frame or mount and get it right. You will have disasters at first, but persevere and you will soon be enjoying your framing!

ONE

Hobby and Small-Scale Framing

Introduction

You do not need to have expensive equipment to make a frame, and this section is for those who want to make picture frames on a small scale without the expensive tools and equipment required by a professional or semi-professional framer. I would, however, stress that the same basic framing rules apply, in that you want to produce a frame of high quality. If you are an artist (professional or amateur) who sells works of art, the framing must enhance your work both in appearance and quality. How many art-club exhibitions have you seen with competent and attractive pictures ruined by bad framing? How many sales are lost as a consequence?

This book is divided into clearly marked sections, with all aspects of framing explained in easy-to-follow, step-by-step instructions. So it is recommended that even if you are only making hobby frames you read and refer to the other chapters in the 'Professional' and 'Aspects of Framing' sections, i.e. those concerned with making frames, stretching canvas, tapestries, wash line mounts, etc., as the processes, tips and advice contained therein remain the same whether applied to making one frame or one hundred.

As with other sections in the book, 'Hobby and Small-Scale Framing' firstly covers tools and workspace, then the framing construction, and finally the finish.

Tools and Workspace

The only part of the framing process that involves any dusty mess is the cutting of the moulding, which is performed with a saw. Other than that, a well-protected table will be perfectly adequate. A board of 12mm (½-inch) plywood 122 cm (4 ft) by 91.5 cm (3 ft) would be ideal, with a sheet placed between table and board – you can then cut and trim without fear of ruining the family heirloom!

There follows a list of tools that will be essential to your framing:

Mitre block and tenon saw

This is a beechwood block into which the moulding fits. The tenon saw is held in 45-degree splits on both sides, which guide it while cutting. This is the most basic and traditional means of mitre cutting.

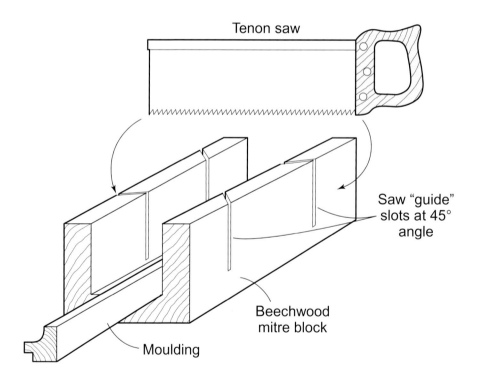

Tenon saw

Saw "guide" slots at 45° angle

Beechwood mitre block

Moulding

Mitre block and tenon saw

Hand mitre saw

This is a saw built into a light metal framework, which holds the saw and has vari-angle settings. These saws range in price from £30-£100 (US$50-$200) and should be your preferred option.

Strap clamp or corner clamp – or both

A strap clamp is a four-corner stay held by a string which is placed around the frame to hold it while the glue dries. (See Equipping Workshop and Setting Up Tools in Section Two for a more detailed explanation and diagram.) The corner clamp is a small screw clamp that holds two pieces of moulding while you pin and glue. While you will definitely need some form of clamp/strap, you can spend as little as £20 (US$35) or as much as £100 (US$200). Tool shops sell a variety of straps and clamps. If you are unsure go for a strap.

Mount (card surround) cutting tool

If you are going to cut a bevelled opening in your mount, you must have a mount-cutting tool of some description for straight, circular or oval mounts. These vary in price from £20 to £100 (US$35-$200), but if this is beyond your budget remember you can buy ready-cut mounts of standard sizes in art shops. However, without one of the patent devices you will not get a mount with that attractive, professional bevelled cut and finish.

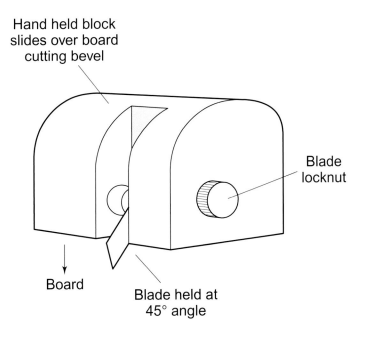

Mount-cutting block

Kraft knife

The Stanley-knife type is best, used with a straight edge. Buy a good-quality straight edge WITH FINGER PROTECTION. Please be aware that kraft knives are very sharp and can inflict fearful wounds.

Additional tools

You will need the following tools to make the frames, many of which you will probably already have in your toolbox:

Panel-pin hammer
Small woodblock approximately 40 x 40 x 60mm (1 x 1 x 2 in.)
Centrepunch to countersink pins
Accurate set square (to check angles of mitres)
Accurate metric or imperial measure/rule
Pencils
Bradawl (for boring holes)
Drill (either hand or electric)
Fine drill bits (the thickness of your panel pins)
Scissors
Pliers (blunt-ended and pointed varieties)
Selection of artist's brushes (No. 2 & No. 4)
Glass-cutter (2mm) (depending on your confidence)
Clean dusters.

Materials Needed

Moulding

This can come from a variety of sources. If you intend using old frames bought from markets or auctions, be on the lookout for woodworm: you do not want to introduce woodworm to your home or, worse still, someone else's! Lengths can also be obtained from a picture-framing shop, moulding wholesaler or from DIY stores and builders' merchants.

Mount board

Card for decorative effect – from craft shops, art shops or framing retailers/wholesalers.
Backing – thin (2mm) hardboard, MDF board, foam core board – from framers or craft suppliers.

Glass

You require 2mm picture-framing glass – either clear, non-reflecting or UV-protecting – which can be obtained from a framer's or glazier's. You can buy the glass ready-cut to size (ask the glazier to de-edge it for your safety, at least until you are confident in handling it), or by the sheet if you want to cut it yourself.

Additional materials

Brown gum-strip paper (50mm/2in.-wide rolls)
Masking tape (25mm/1in.-wide rolls)
Double-sided tape (20mm/ ¾in.-wide rolls)
PVA wood glue (interior, NOT the waterproof variety)
Artists' acrylic paints (for touching up and decorating)
Panel pins – from 20mm/¾in. to 40mm/1¾in.
Rings or screw eyes
Wire/string for hanging
Glass-cleaning liquid (non-smear variety).

Sourcing Your Moulding

First you will have to find a source for your moulding. Here are a few suggestions:

Moulding wholesalers

These companies are the professional picture framer's trade suppliers but most now have a trade counter where they sell to the general public – at a price!

The professionals get their discount through bulk buying so if you have a friend who makes frames or you belong to an art club, consider one person buying the moulding for a group so you can all benefit from a bulk discount. This could apply to all your materials.

DIY stores or from picture framers

Both of the above will often provide a cutting service, leaving you to assemble the frames. This will get you a perfect mitre and can be a very good idea.

Builders' merchants

Builders' merchants carry a range of mouldings used in the carpentry trade. Some of the moulding may be ornate architrave or coving and may not be rebated (the rebate is a recess in the moulding designed to take the picture). This can be overcome by attaching a batten to form a rebate (see 'Cutting, assembling and decorating' in the 'Making the Frame' section opposite). Plain wood frames are ideal if you want to decorate your frames.

Second-hand frames

From junk shops, skips, markets – there are always frames around old pictures that have been disposed of as fashions change. These can be great fun simply to renovate and reuse, but remember the warning mentioned earlier: old frames can be infested with woodworm. Watch for the telltale holes and the sawdust-like powder that indicates activity.

Making the Frame

As mentioned in the introduction, it is strongly recommended that you read the relevant chapters in the Professional section of this book. Apart from the fact that, as an amateur, you will be using hand tools instead of the machinery used by professionals, the same procedures generally apply – so you may find that some of the explanations given in that section are useful.

Measuring the picture

Your first task is to decide the size of your frame. Is your picture to be close-framed or framed with a mount? If the answer is the former, the size of the picture will decide the size of your frame. Allow a loose fit (for expansion and contraction of the picture) and make the frame slightly larger than the picture. You do not want to make a frame and discover the picture does not fit – trust me, it happens!

Your other option is a mounted picture, i.e., a picture with a decorative surround, usually behind glass. For this, measure the picture then decide on the width of the mount. The balance and size of the mount is vital to prevent the presentation looking out of kilter, unbalanced or crushed into the frame; the latter is a common fault when pictures have been fitted into an existing frame and the mount trimmed to compensate for incompatible dimensions. Having decided on the mount dimensions, add them to the picture size, not forgetting to double the width and the height. Thus a 3-inch mount will add 6 inches to both the length and the width.

Cutting, assembling and decorating the frame

If you are using decorative moulding from a builders' merchant, and you need to form a rebate, buy some 10 x 40mm (⅜ x 1¾ in.) batten and glue it under the moulding, secured by masking tape until the glue has dried (normally this takes about 24 hours).

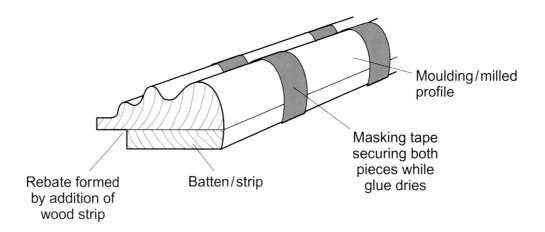

Moulding/milled profile

Masking tape securing both pieces while glue dries

Rebate formed by addition of wood strip

Batten/strip

Moulding and batten

Take your length of moulding and offer it up to the jig or saw base, then trim off the end to 45 degrees. This will give you your first mitre. Measure and mark off the length on the inside of the rebate and carefully cut the moulding to the mark. This will give you your first length.

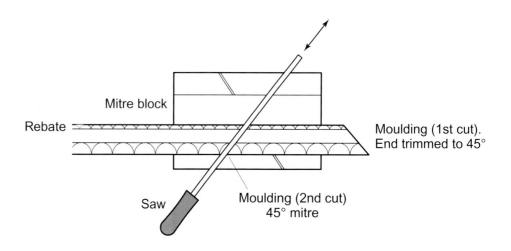

Mitre block

Rebate

Moulding (1st cut). End trimmed to 45°

Saw

Moulding (2nd cut) 45° mitre

Trimming moulding (1st & 2nd cuts)

Trim the moulding again to get the next mitre.

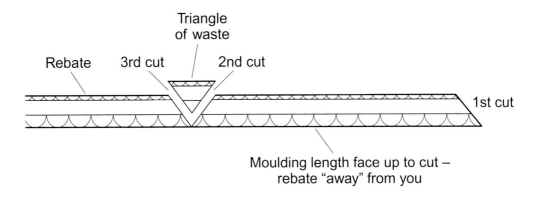

First length cut

To get the second identical length, place the moulding beside the first length and mark off exactly where to cut. Cut the second length. Your two lengths must be exact to ensure your frame is square!

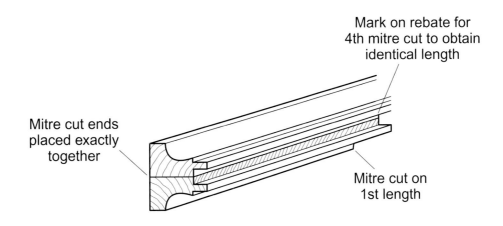

Mitre-cut ends placed exactly together

Repeat the process for the second pair of lengths/sides. You should now have the four sides of your frame. With the set square, check that your mitres are accurate.

String-clamp method

Open up your string clamp so that it is larger than the frame. Place the four sides of moulding on the bench and adjust the string clamp around the frame. Pull tight and double-check that all is well. This is where you must be self-critical. If the mitres do not close together perfectly redo them, because you will never get a perfect joint with inaccurate cuts. Once you are satisfied, release the string clamp and carefully remove one length. Smear a thin layer of glue to both ends then carefully replace. Repeat with the opposite length, so that all four joints will now be glued. Close up the string clamp under tension. Once this has been done, resist the temptation to fiddle with it: any tampering at this stage will impair the glue joint (PVA wood glue dried under pressure will form a joint stronger than the wood itself). Leave the frame to dry for a minimum of 24 hours before removing the clamp.

Once it has dried and been removed from the clamp, the frame will have to be pinned on each mitre. Working in rotation, pre-drill a small hole then tap in your panel pin and countersink slightly. The countersink hole can be filled and touched up later, but if you are very neat you can leave them: being on the side or spine of the moulding, they will not show.

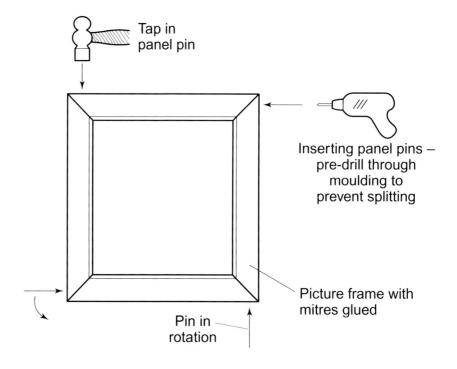

Drill and pin corners

Corner clamps

If you are using a corner clamp, insert a length and width of moulding and screw down the clamps to hold the two pieces. Check that they are a snug and accurate fit. Remove one length, apply a thin smear of glue over the joint, and replace in the clamp. Drill and pin the corner and leave to dry.

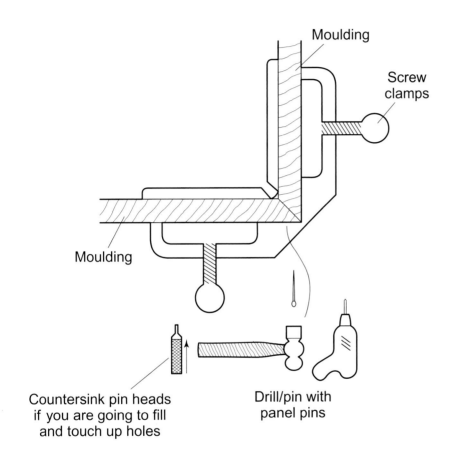

Moulding

Screw clamps

Moulding

Countersink pin heads
if you are going to fill
and touch up holes

Drill/pin with
panel pins

Corner/mitre clamp

Now take the second pair of lengths, insert them into the clamp and repeat the process, making sure that they are in the same way as the first pair so that the two halves of your frame marry up!

Once the pair of 'L's you have made is dry, fix together in the clamp using the same method.

If you only have one clamp, it is worth taking time over the joints to allow them to dry under pressure – 12 hours is sufficient. You will now have your made-up frame.

If you are using commercially produced moulding that is pre-decorated, your joint will have to be left. If you try to touch up the face of this type of moulding, you are more likely to give it a botched appearance. The quality of your mitre joint is thus very important. Take care and with practise you will get a good joint. On the commercially produced moulding, it might be wise to have a framer trim it to size for you. His guillotine will produce an almost invisible joint. On the other hand, if you are using a plain-wood moulding that you intend to decorate (I would recommend this to any hobby framer), you can fill the mitres before painting and decorating.

Decorating the frame

The simplest way to decorate your frame is to paint it with acrylic paints (usually a colour that complements and enhances the picture). However, there are three basic ways to decorate your frame:

1. Stain the wood with wood stain, then varnish
2. Paint the frame with acrylic paint (I don't recommend anyone to use paints that might contain toxic solvents. They are not good for you, so avoid them.)
3. Ornament the frame. There are limitless ideas for decorating the frame with all kinds of objects and textures. For example, a seascape might be enhanced by a frame with seashells glued to it. There are various cold-cure modelling clays that can be used to model and stick objects such as leaves or flowers to the frame.

Don't be afraid to experiment. You will have disasters, but nothing ventured...!

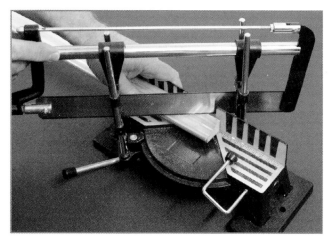

1. Trim off end of moulding with mitre saw.

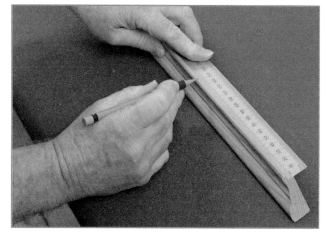

2. Measure and mark the first length for mitre cut.

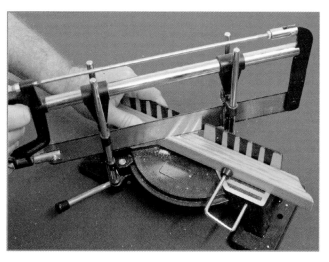

3. Cut second mitre.

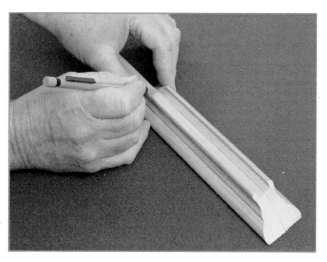

4. Using first length measure off and mark second length to get perfect match.

5. Cut second length – repeat process for other two sides.

6. The four sides of the frame cut and ready for assembly.

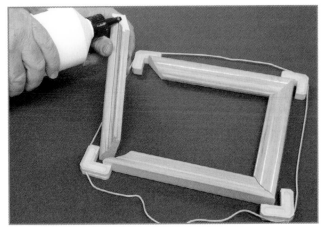

7. Arrange the "string clamp" and spread a thin layer of PVA interior wood glue on mitres.

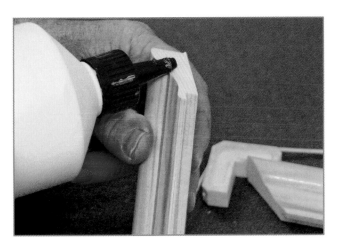

8. Spread a thin layer of glue.

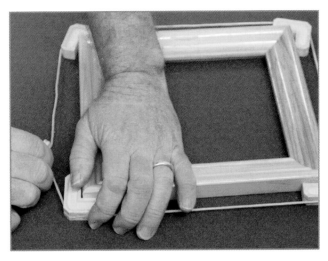

9. Adjust the string clamp.

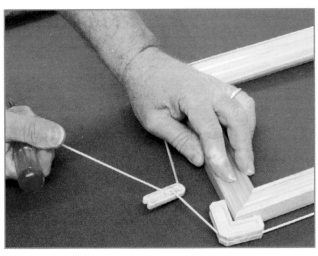

10. Tension the clamp to ensure frame dries under pressure – wrap the string around a screwdriver or other implement/moulding off-cut to increase your leverage.

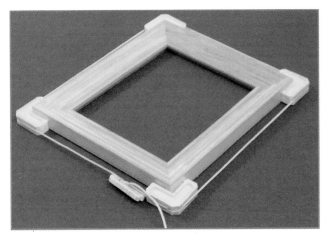

11. Frame clamped and left overnight for glue to dry.

12. Pre-drill and tap in panel pins (always work in rotation).

13. Using centre punch make sure panel pins are flush or just below the surface – and fill the holes to mask the pins (optional).

Finishing the Frame

Finishing a basic frame

If the picture requires only simple framing, i.e., nothing more than a frame around it, you can now check that it fits. If you are happy with the fit, place the picture on top of your chosen backing board – be it 2mm hardboard, MDF, foam core board or pulp board – and trace the outline of the picture onto the board. Cut out with the Stanley knife and insert both picture and board into the frame. Pin in place and tape up. (See pinning and taping methods on pages 21 and 22).

Finishing a frame with mount and glass

The mount (a coloured card surrounding the picture) is designed to enhance the picture and separate it from the glass, with its attendant condensation problem. For this reason, the mount is especially important in Britain's wet climate. You can buy your mount board from an art or craft shop, you can bulk-buy it from framing wholesalers, or you can buy it from framers who will also cut it for you. There are also ready-cut mounts of standard size that you can buy from art shops and some framers.

It takes patience, practice and great care when cutting your mount to achieve the result you want, i.e. a straight, even surround, with a bevelled edge on the picture opening. In this regard, there are several patent cutting systems for the hobby framer. The simplest I know of is the Dexter Matt Cutter, a simple metal block which holds a blade at a 45-degree angle. You place a straight edge between two predetermined points and slide the Dexter along. Repeated on all sides, this produces a very professional finish. You can also cut out the aperture using a Kraft knife, although bear in mind that this will produce a straight not a bevel cut, and so will not look as good.

The basic system to follow is first to cut out the card to the *outer* dimension. Then on the reverse side, using pencil and rule, work out where the *inner* cut is to be made. Having established this, make four fine pinholes in the corners. Turn the board good side up and cut out your aperture using your pinholes as a guide. If you are using one of the patent devices, follow the instructions, as each has varying advice. For a double or triple mount, follow the procedure outlined above, first marking and cutting the card to produce the various layers of mount, then fixing them together with great care – ensuring they are straight and accurate – with a strip of double-sided tape along and behind the top border.

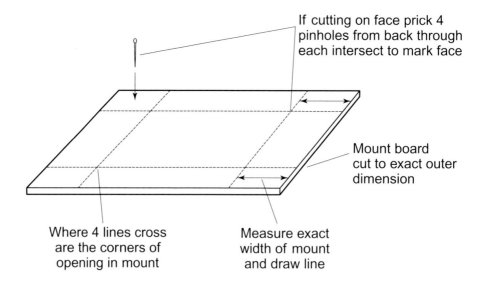

If cutting on face prick 4 pinholes from back through each intersect to mark face

Mount board cut to exact outer dimension

Where 4 lines cross are the corners of opening in mount

Measure exact width of mount and draw line

Cutting mount board

For more complex mounts and wash line mounts, please refer to the appropriate chapters in the Professional section.

HAND CUTTING MOUNT

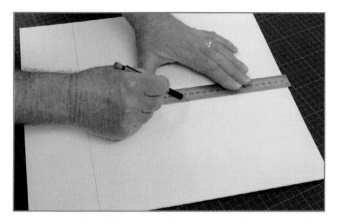 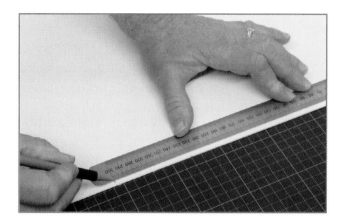

1 & 2. Measure and mark outer dimensions of mount board on <u>rear</u> surface, this must be <u>very</u> accurate.

3. Carefully trim board to size.

4. Using dividers mark out the width of the mount (i.e. the outer to the inner cut which will surround the picture).

5. Mark/connect with fine pencil lines.

6. The mount board ready for 'bevel' cutting (I always use dividers to reduce the risk of mistake!).

7. Using a fine pin mark the four corners to show where to cut on the mount board face (this is ONLY if you are using a cutting block that works from the face, i.e. Dexter matt cutter). If you have the variety that cuts from the rear, this is unnecessary.

8. Cut out the centre using your lines as guides. **N.B.** I have used an inexpensive patent cutter for this. You can use a Kraft knife but you will find the results far from satisfactory.

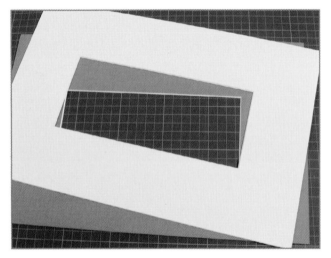

9. The mounts/matts cut and ready.

Glass and glass-cutting

It goes without saying that glass must be handled with care – it can be dangerous. I would strongly recommend that you have your local glazier cut your glass to size for you. Also, ask them to de-edge it to make it safe to handle. If, however, you want to cut your own, you will require a good glass-cutter and a single layer of blanket on your cutting table.

Practise your cutting. The secret is to remember, firstly, to run the wheel over the cut line just *once*, exerting the right pressure so that the wheel *sings* as it runs. Once you have scoured the glass, take the sheet to the edge of the table, placing the scour line just past the edge, and apply a quick, firm push. Remember: nothing violent. If scoured correctly, the glass will snap cleanly along the line. Please be patient with this. Glass-cutting is a skill, just like riding a bicycle: it takes time to perfect, but once mastered it is never forgotten. (Don't forget to wear eye protection to guard against flying splinters/shards.)

Backing

This is the final element you'll need to make your frame. The finish on the back is very important, especially if you are framing your artwork to sell, so take care to choose the right material.

The easiest method for backing is to use the sheet of glass as your template, tracing it onto your backing sheet, which is then cut out with your Stanley knife and straight edge. It is a good idea, if not essential practice, to place a sheet of card under the board to be cut to act as a cushion for the knife. Also, have a special cutting board of 1cm-thick ply, which when damaged can be inverted and eventually replaced.

Assembling the frame

Having cut and prepared the component parts, first clean the glass in the frame on both sides, ensuring all smears and dust are removed. Cover with the backing and prepare the picture. This will entail fixing it to the mount using double-sided tape. Make sure the picture is straight, and only fix along the top edge (to prevent cockling, the picture should be able to expand and contract, so fixing on one edge only leaves three edges for movement). Place the mounted picture in the frame, again checking for dust. (if you have a vacuum cleaner with an extension hose and a clean brush, use this to remove dust from the glass.)

Pinning

Now pin the back in place using the following method. Take the small wooden block mentioned in the Tools section and put it against the moulding (this will absorb impact shock from the hammer, thus protecting the frame). Place a 20mm panel pin up against the rebate and hold in place – thumb round block, fingers on backing, one finger on the pin – and with the hammer tap in one third of its length. Repeat near each corner.

With the contents now held, turn over and check once again that the glass is free of dust on the interior and that the picture and mount are straight. If you are unsure of your judgement, use dividers to check accuracy. Once you are happy that all is as it should be (remember: be critical!), continue pinning the back, inserting panel pins every 80mm (3in.) all round, keeping them evenly spaced and neat.

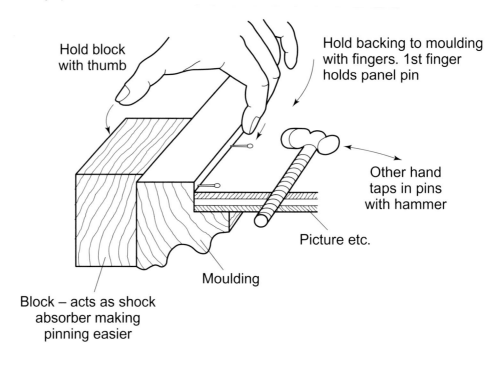

Hold block with thumb

Hold backing to moulding with fingers. 1st finger holds panel pin

Other hand taps in pins with hammer

Picture etc.

Moulding

Block – acts as shock absorber making pinning easier

Pinning with a hammer

Taping

Using strips of moistened paper tape (gum-strip), tape up the back of the frame neatly to protect from dust and insects. Leave taped frame to dry overnight. (Please do not use plastic pre-glued packing tapes: they are difficult to handle, do not look good and in the long term will leave a mess on the frame. Gum-strip tape is easily removed by moistening if you need to open the frame.)

Hangings

Fix hangings by pre-boring holes with a bradawl and screwing in eyes, then tying string or wire between the two. The hanging wire should be fixed at two thirds of the height of the frame (measured from the bottom). Tie the wire or string with care so that it looks neat. Check that the fixings are strong, then your frame is ready to be hung.

TWO

Professional/ Semi-Professional Framing

Introduction

One of the main reasons for writing this section is that, firstly, I am constantly being asked by friends all over the world how they should set themselves up as picture framers. Secondly, and more importantly, I am constantly being told by fellow picture framers that they cannot make really good profits from their framing. I did, so what made me different? It took a while to discover, because I naturally assumed everybody makes the frames the way I do. When I realised the difference it was, as they say, blindingly obvious – I 'mass-produce' my bespoke frames. In using this phrase I am not implying a reduction in the quality of the end product or prostituting the noble art of picture framing. I am merely increasing my productivity, minimising costs and offering customers a deal they rarely refuse!

So when you read this section, please understand that my workshop and methods are all designed to fit this philosophy. If you frame one picture at a time, you can spend anything from 20 or 30 minutes up to several hours on each frame. You will be pushed to produce 20 frames a week, and to make a living each frame will have to be very expensive, which in turn may lose you customers.

I have always found that people on average incomes have to work to budgets; but wealthier people also mind their expenses – that is how many become rich – and the seriously wealthy are few and far between and pursued for their money by large numbers of people. Your ideal clientele will be the middle market – those vast numbers of people who live in the suburbs. To attract this type of customer your price has to be right, along with your quality, which must be perfect and consistent. It is with this attitude that I went into picture framing. I had learnt the craft from experts, but I wanted to make money, so I set out to produce as many frames as possible per week with the minimum of effort and strain on my part, earning as much money as possible in return; no matter how satisfying I find the making of a picture frame, the real pleasure is paying-in at the bank the money that someone has paid for it.

To achieve this high return I decided that my frames should take a matter of approximately 10 minutes each (this was the rate I decided I could manage without the quality suffering). Hence, my method of framing pictures is as follows:

Measure up and produce a job sheet for all the pictures to be framed in the week. Cut all the frames together and then make them; then cut all the mounts together, with the same applying to glass, backing, assembly and finishing.

My framing week is thus comprised of:

Monday

Measure out the various frame sizes that will be needed and write up the week's job sheet. Cut all the mouldings to size and make the first 'L' of the frame (or all the frame depending on your fixing system).

Tuesday

Finish making the frames then cut all the mounts (matts).

Wednesday

Cut all the glass and backing. This will see all the picture-frame components ready. Clean all the glass and leave the frames stacked overnight so the glass can dry.

Thursday

Prepare the pictures, fix them in their mounts, stretch tapestries, trim then work through the final assembly. When they are all stacked and pinned, cut the backing tape and tape up the rears, leaving them to dry overnight.

Friday

Make good any production marks on the moulding spines, fit/fix the hanging furniture, wrap the frames and invoice. Delivery to the shops on Friday afternoon or Saturday morning.

By working in this way, I felt I could far more easily control quality. Breaking the job sheet down into component parts, i.e., cutting all the moulding, mounts or glass at once, you can devote all your attention to that particular task, thus reducing the possibility of making a mistake on the machine or tool you are using; whereas constantly chopping and changing from one tool to another increases the chance of a lapse in concentration and therefore the possibility of making a mistake.

With this method I can produce up to 150 bespoke frames per week; if I have a quiet week with, say, only 20 or so frames, the production is so rapid that I can have a leisure week doing other things!

The other main benefit of this system is the room it affords me to manoeuvre on pricing – I work on the principle of providing quality work at a reasonable price. Applying the same precept, you will find once you become known that you have tapped into a huge market.

As an exercise, just look round your walls. How many framed pictures are there? How many frames have you had made? Did you go back? Did the price take your breath away? Then take a walk around the streets at dusk, the time that lights go on but curtains are not yet drawn. You will be amazed at the blank walls – a vast potential market for picture frames.

As a proportion of the population, people who have large numbers of pictures on their walls are relatively few. There are many more who would like to have pictures framed but do not for often the simplest of reasons – price and the fear of getting 'stung'. I have found that people are often shy about choosing their frames. They do not want to appear ignorant, tasteless or vulgar. It's up to you to make them feel at ease and in control. If you do, your reward will be a satisfied customer who always comes back. The final choice is up to you, but remember if you are in business the idea is to make money. Look at the car industry. Both ordinary cars and luxury cars are mass-produced, both types often on the same production line, one after the other!

To those who would argue that this approach takes the soul or at least the pleasure out of framing, I say try enjoying life when your business is not paying the bills! There is a common belief among framers that you have to be 'arty'. Okay, be arty if you think it helps your image with customers. However, the real secret of being a good framer is giving the customer the frame they want. What you might think is good taste may well be seen by another as simply hideous. So rather than being arty, think of your customers' needs and tastes – remember that they are paying the money and they are the ones who will have to live with your creation! Satisfied customers will come back with more framing jobs while the dissatisfied will take their business elsewhere!

SETTING UP
Why Picture Framing?

You obviously have an interest in picture framing, so now it's time to decide what type of picture framing you want to do. There are three main options:

a. Framing your own pictures as a hobby but not on a commercial basis.
b. Small-scale picture framing in your spare time and for a small profit – often called 'bespoke'.
c. Commercial framing – either 'bespoke', i.e. you frame for the customer on a personal level, or 'trade', i.e. you make picture frames for shops and volume customers.

Bespoke framing is traditionally like bespoke tailoring – the frame is made to the individual customer's requirements. Trade-to-shops framing is bespoke framing using the shopkeeper as your middle man to take orders and deal with the customer, i.e. you supply the samples and he brings in the orders – but to have a viable business you must be able to turn these orders around on a weekly basis!

Trade-to-trade entails the production of huge numbers of very low-priced frames of the kind seen in superstores for cheap prints, photo frames, etc. This for the most part requires power-tooling and factory production, but even so the same basic principles pertaining to bespoke frames also apply here.

At this stage you have to consider two very important questions. Firstly, picture framing is a very 'clean' trade. You are dealing with people's pictures, which may have great monetary value and will certainly more often than not have sentimental value. They really do not want them spoilt. So you have to be a clean worker, someone who is very self-critical and has a keen eye for detail. Secondly, you are going to be working with very sharp tools – guillotines, knives and cutters – all of which require razor-sharp blades. These tools are dangerous and, if you are careless or accident-prone, be warned! This also applies to materials. The edges of 2mm picture glass are notoriously sharp, as are mount and card edges.

Location of Workshop

If you are planning to frame for yourself, it doesn't really matter where you have a workshop – a dry garage or a large garden shed will do perfectly well provided it is not damp and has a strong floor. I started in a 2.5 x 5 m (8 x 16 ft) concrete prefab garden building which I lined and insulated. I still had to keep the glass in a little wooden summer house, and glass cutting became a bit of an ordeal when it snowed, as I had to keep the doors open to cut the glass! But the little prefab, in which I still successfully produced over a hundred frames a week, got me going until I could afford to extend it to 8.5 x 2.5 m (28 x 8 ft).

If you have got the space, start at home until you establish yourself; later you can move to a shop or industrial unit. Whatever kind of workshop you have, it needs to be in a place where customers can park, load their frames and bring in pictures without getting them wet. On more than one occasion I have witnessed a customer bringing an expensive piece of artwork for framing, unprotected, in a deluge of rain! Remember that art and picture framing do not like damp.

Based on my personal experience, I would say an ideal workshop is a space of approximately 9 x 2.75 m (30 x 9 ft). Length is handy, as the framing can be run like a production line, minimising the risk of knocking, gouging or breaking frames. If you don't have a single large space, you may have a bedroom or another room to which you can apportion some aspects of the work. When considering your workshop, bear in mind hazards to customers, such as steps, slopes, slippery surfaces and unguarded equipment. If someone has an accident, you could be liable and in our current blame culture any action against you could turn out to be nasty and expensive. Whatever you do, don't just trust that your household insurance will cover you: make sure you have very good public-liability insurance cover. Finally, and probably most importantly, remember that to tap into a decent-sized potential customer base you need to be accessible to those customers. A picture-framing workshop on a peaceful Welsh mountain will probably not make you much money!

So, in brief, your workshop needs to be:

1. Convenient for work and trade
2. Adequately large to be practical and safe
3. Dry, with an even temperature
4. Accessible.

The other big consideration is noise levels. Power tools can greatly antagonise neighbours, who in turn can bring the environmental health and planning authorities down on you – and they can be very awkward. I once had the experience of finding the perfect location for my business to expand to, a large shop, but the local planning department had other ideas: their response to my application for change of use was that I made picture frames, that the making indicated manufacture, and that therefore I ought to have an industrial unit, not a high-street shop.

Also beware the dreaded Health and Safety inspector when creating potentially harmful dust. The Health and Safety Inspectorate have the power to make your life very miserable, even if you work alone and do not employ anyone. I recently had a visit from a Health & Safety inspector whose missionary zeal sought to protect me from myself!

Design of Workshop

To produce frames successfully with minimum damage to yourself, the frames and other people's works of art, and also for sheer working comfort, your workshop should be very carefully designed bearing in mind the need for possible modifications as your business grows and progresses. As previously mentioned, it must have a dry, even atmosphere. Warped mouldings and mouldy mount board are expensive losses.

I always run a dehumidifier and when closing up at night I regularly spray with insecticide (a fly spray stocked in most supermarkets) to control pests such as the dreaded woodworm. Rats and mice can also be a problem, so make sure they cannot get in!

Your workshop will require storage space for:

1. Moulding
2. Mountboard/Matt board
3. Backing board
4. Glass
5. Hardware
6. Sundries
7. Frames in production
8. Storing customers' artwork
9. Storing finished work.

Work in your workshop will require areas for:

1. Cutting moulding
2. Assembling frames
3. Cutting mount board and backing board, and mount cutting
4. Glass cutting
5. Assembling and finishing.

Storage space for materials

1. Moulding

Moulding comes in 2- and 3-metre lengths and stores away very well high up in the workshop – on crossbars near the ceiling or on wall brackets. You will also need to accommodate offcuts of moulding – plywood bins near the guillotine work well.

2. Mount board

Mount board stores away very well in vertical racks underneath the mount-cutting bench. Again you must allow space for storing offcuts.

3. Backing board

Backing board, of which you will probably have more than one type, can be stored with the mount board or under the glass-cutting table.

4. Glass

Glass will need a vertical rack in a safe position where neither you nor your customers can get injured and from where it can be easily lifted onto the cutting bench. Remember that you will stock two varieties of glass: clear and non-reflective.

5. Hardware

Namely pins, nails, wedges, staples, strut-back assemblies, mirror plates and a myriad of useful accessories. These should be arranged in boxes or in containers on shelves near the workstation where they will be used.

6. Sundries

Kraft paper, tapes, glues, fillers, stains, etc., should all be stored away on racks or shelves that leave them ready to hand.

7. Frames in production

As you make the frames, they will have to be stacked or stored in such a way as to avoid damage during the production process.

8. Storing customers' artwork

This is extremely important. You will need a secure cupboard, drawer or container where works for framing can be stored as safely as possible. Getting insurance cover on them is a good idea, though personally I found this to be very expensive, and some of the companies also demanded Fort Knox-style storage facilities!

9. Storing finished work

You need readily accessible storage where customers' framed work can be kept safely – and removed safely too: there is nothing worse than making a perfect frame for a customer and then damaging it as you give it to them!

Workspace in your workshop

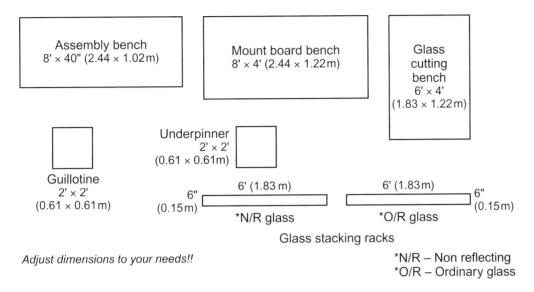

The main card cutouts to plan workshop.

1. Cutting moulding

Guillotines are usually heavy floor-standing foot-operated double-bladed mitre cutters that require a clear run of 3 metres to the left for the moulding length and anything up to 3 metres to the right for the cut pieces of moulding. On the couple of occasions when I have had to make frames requiring lengths of more than 2 metres, I found it easier to move the guillotine to accommodate the extra length.

2. Assembling frames

Assembling the frames is done either on a framers' vice or more commonly with an underpinner, which can be either free-standing or bench-mounted.

3. Cutting mount board, etc.

For cutting mount board and backing board, I have always used a bench dedicated to the purpose, with a mount-cutting machine at one end and a card-cutting guillotine at the other, and with card and board storage underneath.

4. Glass-cutting

Once again, I have always used a dedicated bench for glass-cutting, one that is lower than the other benches and more robustly built, with a soft top to protect the glass.

5. Assembling and finishing

This is a most important, long and spacious bench covered in soft protection to prevent scratching, and with space underneath for a powerful cylinder vacuum cleaner to ensure dust-free assembly.

Dry-mounting benches and presses are not dealt with here as I have not found them necessary in 25 years of framing (but see the section on dry mounting in 'Aspects of Framing').

Before you start building your workshop it helps to draw a plan so as to work out the best possible location of benches. This is very important; a chaotic workshop will not inspire confidence in your customers. The first requirement is to measure the rooms/spaces you are using and draw them to scale on a sheet of paper – graph paper is very useful for this.

1. Assembly bench – 2.5m x 1m (8 x 3ft 3in.) - ideal but 1.8m x 1m (6 x 3ft 3in.) will do.
2. Mount cutting table – 2.5m x 1.2m (8 x 4ft) - possibly with 20cm (8in.) extra length for large mount/matt cutter.
3. Glass-cutting table – 1.8m x 1.2m (6 x 4ft), large enough to take sheet of glass.
4. Mitre guillotine – 60 x 60cm (2 x 2ft)
5. Free-standing underpinner – 60 x 60cm (2 x 2ft)
6. Stack of glass along wall – 1.5m x 15cm (5 ft x 6in.).

Once you have the outline of the workshop on paper, draw to the same scale on a separate sheet or a coloured card the worksurfaces in the plan, i.e., the benches and large tools, and cut them out. Now you can move the different benches around the proposed workshop to find the most suitable layout.

1. Assembly bench

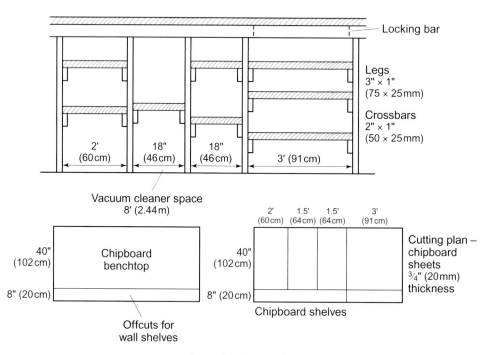

Assembly bench plan

The assembly bench is the bench where you will probably spend the most time. Its size will be determined by what you expect your largest frame to be. I always work to an outside measurement of 90cm x 1.5m (3 x 5ft). You will rarely have a frame more than 60 x 90cm (2 x 3ft), so the extra dimension gives you room to move. On this assumption, your minimum work area needs to be 1.02m x 1.83m (3ft 4in. x 6ft). Approximately 30cm (1ft) in from the left-hand side of your bench (or the right-hand side if you are left-handed) screw a 50 x 25mm (2 x 1in.) batten the full width of the bench, i.e., front to rear. This bar will act as a brake when you are tapping or firing fixing pins or darts into the moulding to close the back of the picture frame. The stop bar holds the frame while you apply pressure to the back.

The assembly bench needs as many padded shelves as possible underneath, so that you can stack frames under construction, plus a space for a powerful cylinder/drum vacuum cleaner. The best shelf-paddings are the coarse dark-grey blankets which you can get in surplus stores, but any blanket that is not fluffy is fine. The blanket should be stretched over and stapled to the bench to provide a non-scratch surface.

2. Mount-cutting table

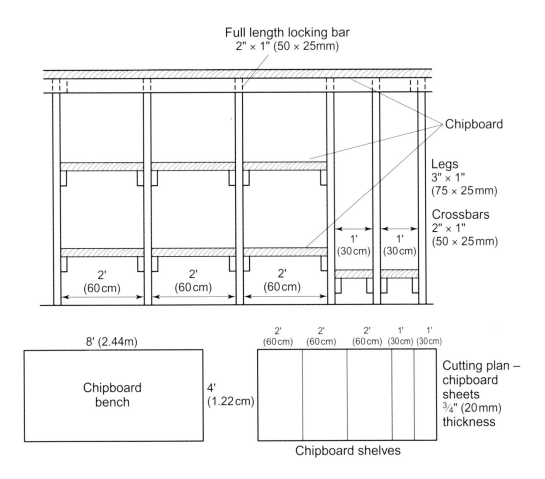

Mount-cutting bench plan

The size of this table will depend on what size of mount-cutting machine you choose. I always choose the largest and best! You may, however, elect to use one of the hand-operated mount cutters, and if so you won't need this bench. The best solution in that case is to increase the size of your assembly bench. The same also applies to the bench-end guillotine for cutting backing board and mount board: a lot of framers prefer simply to use a steel straight edge and a Stanley knife. The choice is yours.

Should you choose to go for the mat/mount-cutting machine and bench-end guillotine, then a 2.5 x 1.2m (8 ft x 4ft) table utilising a single sheet of 20 mm (¾in.) chipboard will be ideal for 1120 x 815mm (44 x 32in.) Double Imperial mount board.

3. Glass-cutting table

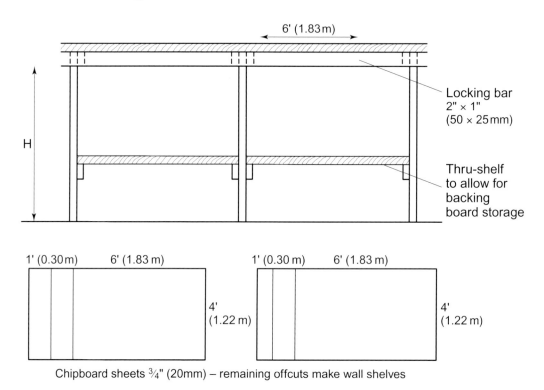

Glass-cutting bench plan

This must be a minimum of 1.8 x 1.2m (6 x 4ft) to accommodate the glass sheets. It has to be firm/sturdy and have at least two shelves underneath for the flat storage of backing board. MDF/hardboard are relatively heavy materials whose weight when stacked on the shelves will give the glass cutting table stability.

To protect the glass, many people use a blanket, but the ideal material is 20mm (¾in.) insulating fibreboard or softboard laid shiny surface up. It is easy to change when it wears, but in any case a single slab on the table will last many years. It is also very easy to keep clean of glass fragments, which otherwise are liable to put scratches in your glass. You can also turn this table into a general workbench for the occasional screwing or rough work that you might have to carry out by simply lifting off the soft protection.

4. Mitre guillotine

These can be either hand or foot-operated, I strongly recommend the free-standing foot-operated models. They are quick, efficient and a pleasure to use. Their actual base area is around 60 x 60cm (2 x 2ft) with support arms on two sides.

5. Free-standing underpinner

A free-standing underpinner is set on a base of approximately 60 x 60cm (2 x 2ft) and is pedal-operated. It can also be bench-mounted or fixed to a wall. I like the free-standing model as this can be moved to accommodate awkward frame dimensions.

6. Glass stacking

The norm when buying glass is to purchase 25 sheets of clear at a time and maybe 10 sheets of non-reflecting. For every sheet of non-reflecting you use, you will probably use 50 sheets of clear. Non-reflecting is not popular and tends to be used for photos or pictures that will experience a light problem where the picture is to be hung. There is also the new UV-resistant glass for protecting pictures.

Allow a wall space for the glass of approximately l.5m x 15cm (5ft x 6in.), which should also be easily accessible for carrying and lifting glass onto the cutting table. 2mm glass is easily broken and very sharp, and hence dangerous; so pre-plan any carrying or lifting with great care and ensure the glass stack is well away from public or occasional access.

Having decided on the size of the benches and machines you are going to install, make your card cut-outs and spend time arranging your workshop. Then using a measure make sure you can work and move between the benches and machines easily and unobstructed. Remember that you will be carrying frames and other objects, so don't cramp yourself.

Once you have designed your workshop and made the benches, you will then need to design all necessary storage and hanging facilities around the benches and work areas for ease of access.

Constructing Your Workshop

The following is the method I have used to set up three framing workshops over the last 25 years, each of which worked extremely well and was reasonably inexpensive to install. My last picture-framing workshop, which I set up in 1998, cost £4,000 – and that was with all the best equipment, timber and board to build the fixtures and fittings, as well as a very good range of stock.

Benches

The first consideration when making your workbenches is to figure out the height of each bench. For assembly and mount-cutting benches, you will need to be able to stand comfortably upright. Close your eyes and imagine yourself working on a frame, putting your hands in front of you as if you were working – make sure you are comfortable. Measure the distance from immediately below your hands to the floor. This will give you the ideal bench-top height. For example, I am 1.85m (6ft 1in.) tall and I work on benches with a top height of 99cm (39in.).

Glass-cutting is different as you need to lean over to run the cutter over the glass. To determine this height, stand comfortably and imagine cutting with your arms down, then measure the distance from below your hands to the floor. Once again as a guide, I have the bench worktop set at 89cm (35in.) off the floor.

Spending hours working over a surface that is too low will play havoc with your back, so as you are the main worker in the workshop fit the benches for yourself. If necessary, should you take on someone to help out, you can always make adjustments.

Having decided on the position and height of the benches, the fun really starts when you make them! For making the workshop that I have illustrated (i.e. with three main workbenches) you will need the following:

1. 20 mm chipboard 2.5 x 1.2m (8 x 4ft) – 6 sheets
2. 75 x 25mm (3 x 1in.) whitewood PAR* – 44m (141ft)
3. 50 x 25mm (2 x 1in.) whitewood PAR* – 74m (242ft)

*PAR = planed all round

The above whitewood/pine is the minimum requirement for the benches, framing rack and shelving. To be safe, order an extra 15m (50ft) of each – it will always be used. The benches are made on the principle of a series of pine 'ladders' onto which you fit the 20mm chipboard tops and shelving.

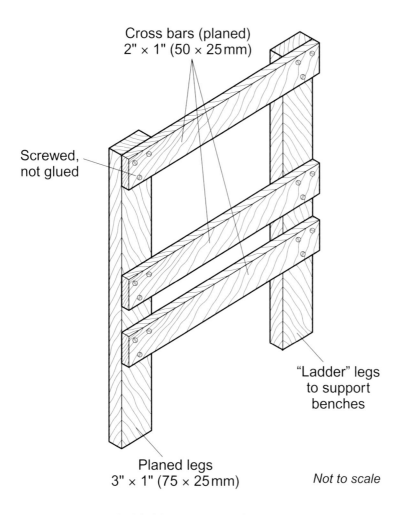

Cross bars (planed)
2" × 1" (50 × 25mm)

Screwed,
not glued

"Ladder" legs
to support
benches

Planed legs
3" × 1" (75 × 25mm)

Not to scale

'Ladder' legs to support benches

First of all, cut your 75 × 25mm (3 × 1in.) legs for the bench, using the height requirement you calculated, minus the thickness of the chipboard top. Then using a right-angle square, accurately screw on the 50 × 25mm (2 × 1in.) cross bars, which have to be precut to the width of the bench minus 38mm (1½in.) to accommodate the two long 50 × 25mm (2 × 1in.) locking bars.

Remember when you buy planed timber that it is narrower than the size stated, as the measurement is made on sawn timber. Planing removes about 8mm (¼in.), so 50 × 25mm (2 × 1in.) planed is in reality, 45 × 20mm (1¾in × ¾in.). Allow for this in your calculations.

To ensure that you have level shelves, each set of ladder cross bars should correspond to their opposite number. Once you have made the legs/ladders, fix the long locking bars to front and rear and move the bench to its final destination. Check your levels, and, once satisfied, fix the bench structure to the wall.

Chipboard

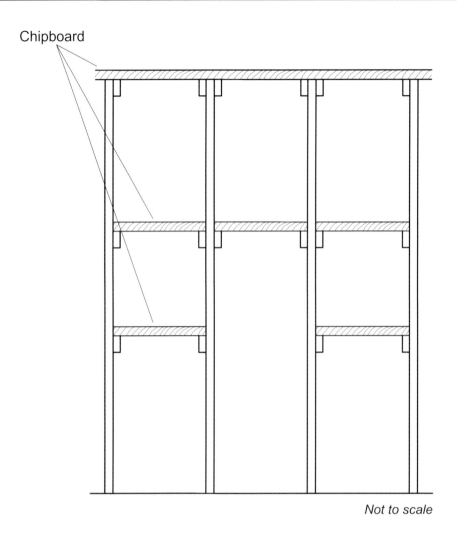

Not to scale

Cross bars on legs with chipboard shelving

Having fixed the structure to the wall, cut and fit the chipboard and screw it down. Bearing in mind that your requirements in the workshop will inevitably change, always use screws so that dismantling and reassembling the workbenches will be relatively easy.

Shelving

The offcuts of chipboard should make six large shelves that can be fitted above the workbenches. I recommend you fix them using the white or grey pressed-steel shelving brackets that are readily available in supermarkets and DIY stores. A length of 50 x 25mm (2 x 1in.) screwed to the front edge stiffens the shelf and makes a very good anchor point for clips and hooks from which to hang tools so that they are ready to hand.

These brackets also make ideal stacking systems for moulding. First, arrange three or four brackets on the wall to support the lenghts of moulding – I work on three brackets for 2-metre lengths or four brackets for 3-metre lengths of moulding. Then screw a 30cm (12in.) offcut of 50 x 25mm (2 x 1in.) batten to the bracket, stapling offcuts of blanket around the wooden batten to cushion the moulding.

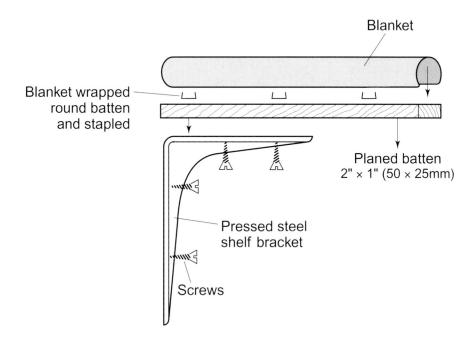

Blanketed moulding racking

Taking a shelf bracket, screw a 12-, 14- or 16-inch length of 50 x 25mm (2 x 1in.) to the bracket, cover the wood in blanket offcuts and fix these individual brackets on spare wall space – they are very useful for hanging frames that are not immediately required. You will find that you get pictures to redo which are sometimes in very attractive, perfectly good frames that the clients do not want, and you can always hang these away to be used later on other pictures or else to be restored. I used to make the picture frames for a large brewery. Their interior designers would say, for instance, that they were renovating a Victorian pub and wanted pictures to suit – many of those old discarded frames now hang in pubs around the country. However, with old frames be mindful of the dreaded woodworm!

Lighting and workshop electrics

You will need very good lighting for the workshop. I have always used 1.2m (4ft) fluorescent (neon) tubes mounted above every bench to give excellent overhead light. I also have a 90cm (3ft) tube mounted on the shelf over the assembly bench to boost the lighting when I'm finishing frames or doing fine work. I have power points to the rear or to the side of all benches and also on the front of the assembly bench. Bear in mind that is now illegal for amateurs to do anything more than minor electrical work themselves. You will certainly need to use a qualified electrician to fit out your workshop with the necessary lighting and power outlets.

The modern picture-frame wholesalers tend to supply everything you could wish for and more, including all the fittings and ready-made workbenches, although I would recommend you build your own benches. It saves you money, and you will also have a workspace custom-made exactly to your requirements, which will vary according to your ongoing requirements. The same applies with storage. Do you keep your screw eyes, mirror plates, pins and hardware in expensive purpose-made stacking systems or, as I have always done, in labelled plastic food containers and old jam-jars. My tapes hang on homemade racks, and the Kraft-paper dispenser is two pressed-steel brackets, two offcuts of 75 x 25mm (3 x 1in.) and an old wooden curtain pole. The brackets cost me £1 and the dispenser has seen years of service and still looks good! Ultimately, the choice of the size and style of workshop and what you equip it with is yours – whether that means you buy the various things you need ready-made or you opt for a money-saving but highly professional DIY workshop. You could say buying everything ready-made saves time, but to build the workshop I have described can take less than a week – and that at a leisurely pace. What is more, standing back and looking at what you have built at the end of the process is extremely satisfying!

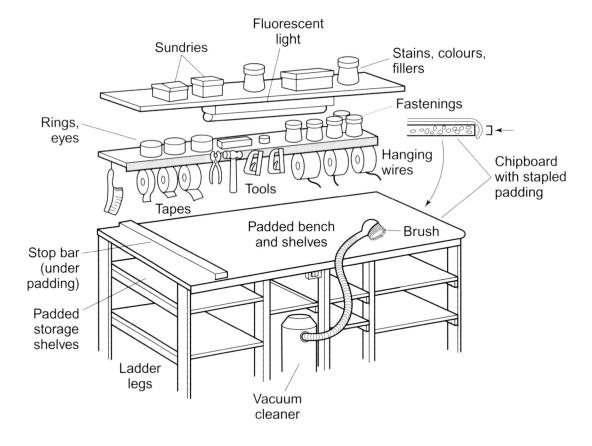

Fluorescent light

Sundries

Stains, colours, fillers

Fastenings

Rings, eyes

Chipboard with stapled padding

Hanging wires

Tools

Tapes

Stop bar (under padding)

Padded bench and shelves

Brush

Padded storage shelves

Ladder legs

Vacuum cleaner

The assembly bench

Equipping the Workshop & Setting Up Tools

1. Mitre guillotine

Having committed yourself to buying the equipment, you will first of all need a machine to cut mouldings. Unless you are a small-time hobby framer, don't even think of mitre boxes, saws and shooting blocks for planing your joints: a professional guillotine produces a join that is so fine as to be virtually invisible.

Guillotines all work on the same principle of needing a base or tabletop upon which the moulding rests. Adjustable, sliding rebate supports prevent the pressure of the blades crushing the unsupported rebate (or 'rabbit' as the old-time framers called it), which is the part of the frame the glass, picture and backing fit into. A heavy triangular block slides through the base moved by a spring-loaded foot pedal. Attached to the head is a pair of blades at right angles to one another and at 45 degrees to the base. The block also moves backwards and forwards, so in essence your moulding is placed on the table. The rebate faces away towards the blades, and the spine rests on the vertical shoulders at the front of the machine. The rebate supports slide under the rebate. The block is then moved away so that the blade, moving up and down, takes a small wedge cut out of the moulding. It is then moved in progressively until the moulding is 'nibbled' or cut through. The final 'click' of the blades makes a fine cut to give you a perfect double mitre.

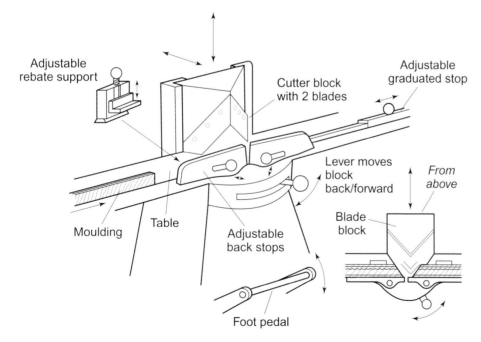

Moulding mitre guillotine

The guillotine will be supplied with comprehensive instructions. It is a simple machine and with a few hours' practice you will soon be cutting perfect frames. The machine will be calibrated to facilitate the measurement of the moulding you are cutting. Its various settings are also very precisely calibrated.

There are several very good makes of guillotine. Apart from the foot-operated ones, there are also hand-operated bench models, which are fine for the hobby framer though I would not recommend them for a professional. There are also pneumatic models, which are very expensive but worth considering if you are making literally many hundreds of frames each week or if you have some physical disability that would make it difficult for you to use any other kind of guillotine. But be aware that going pneumatic will hugely increase your set-up costs.

You will need two other important items to go with your guillotine. The first is a very accurate set square to check the accuracy of machine and moulding cuts. The other is some form of collecting box for the moulding shavings, which accumulate in volume and unrestrained can be a real nuisance underfoot. These collected shavings burn very nicely in a pot-bellied stove – quite handy to heat the home or workshop!

2. Underpinner

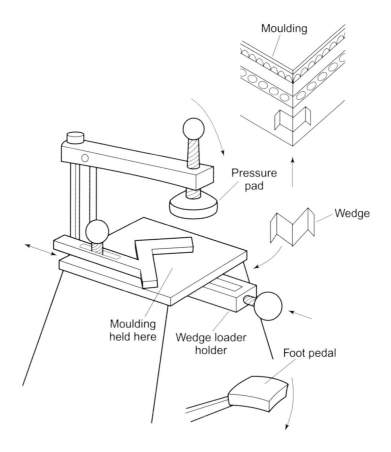

Underpinner

In the order of making frames, your next requirement is to join the moulding pieces together.

The current most popular form of fixing is an underpinner. This is basically a foot-operated machine which pushes the pieces of moulding to be joined into the holding bracket. When foot pressure is applied, a padded press descends and holds the moulding fast while a W-shaped steel wedge is forced into the base. Two of these are normally inserted a given distance apart. They can also be stacked, i.e., one pushed in after another, forming a 'pillar' of fixings through the thickness of the moulding.

The only drawback I have found with the underpinners I have used is that the PVA white resin glue I use requires pressure to form a very strong joint. I don't feel the underpinner produces the required pressure, so I use a clamping system to increase the strength of the joints. The advantage of the underpinner is its speed, and the way it applies fixings also means there is no making good on the spine of the moulding to cover pin- or nail-holes.

Once again there are hand-operated underpinners or pneumatic ones, and the same comments apply to these as to guillotines.

3. Framer's vices and clamps

The traditional fixing method for moulding is to use a framer's vice, pinning the joints in rotation.

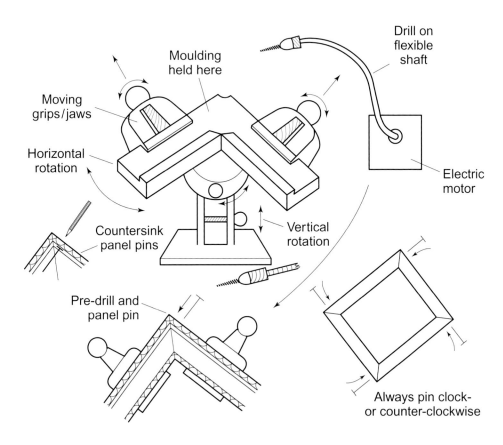

Picture framer's vice

The framer's vice is a traditional design with two clamps at right angles to take two sides of the frame and with ample space to pin or glue the ends. The vice rotates through 180 degrees and raises or lowers the angle of the frame through 90 degrees to get the best-possible work position. I have always had one of these vices and consider it the best all-round tool I possess.

With this vice I have a small electric motor that powers a flexible drill shaft holding a drill bit for pre-drilling the moulding. The drill bit is very fine so as to minimise the risk of the panel pins splitting the wood. There are numerous fixing methods, all based on clamps that pull tight round the frame, which then requires pinning once the glue has dried. There are two types of clamps that I have found are both efficient and cheap.

The first is the Stanley string-frame clamp, comprised of a nylon cord with a plastic lock and four moulded 90-degree corners. These are put round the frame and tensioned, then the joints are adjusted for a perfect fit. To increase tension, I use a moulding offcut to take up the extra cord and pull very hard. You can then underpin the frame so it is fixed and dried under pressure.

In the old days, framers used to get old bedsprings, cut them to form a C-shape, sharpen the ends and use these to clamp the moulding while the glue dried. Ulmia clamps are an Italian clamp system based on the same idea. They are sharpened C-shaped tensile steel springs of different sizes which are applied to the spine of the moulding using special pliers. They do damage the spine, but proper making good gets over this problem. Especially in the case of mouldings of large dimensions, this system makes life very much easier.

There is in fact a huge variety of clamping systems available with new designs coming on the market every year. The best advice I can offer on clamping is to keep it simple.

4. Mount cutters

The next machine you will need is a mount cutter. The mount is the coloured card that forms a border around the picture. The opening is cut all around with a bevelled edge, and the best way to do this is to get a purpose-made machine. These machines work on the principle of a baseboard with graduated stops on which you place the mount board face down. A long hinged arm is then lowered, on which is a running rail with a sliding block. This block holds a blade for cutting through the mount board. With care and practice you will learn how to cut a perfect mount with this machine, turning out mounts in volume quickly, painlessly and accurately.

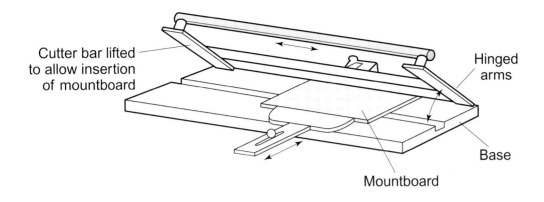

Cutter bar lifted to allow insertion of mountboard

Hinged arms

Base

Mountboard

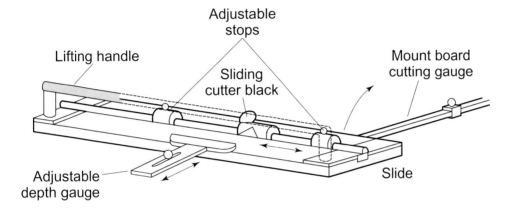

Lifting handle

Adjustable stops

Sliding cutter black

Mount board cutting gauge

Adjustable depth gauge

Slide

Mount-cutting machine

The alternative to a machine is mount-cutting by hand. For this you will find there are various blocks and knives available. I find them slow and tedious, but they are fine for the hobby framer.

There are also oval mount-cutting machines. These are very expensive and in my experience give very little return: after 25 years of framing I still get very few oval orders! The main machines for oval-cutting are either a micrometre mounted blade on an arm that describes an oval, or a blade on a fixed arm that rests on a base that moves in an oval, thereby cutting the board (or piece of glass, which can be useful) in that shape.

I would suggest leaving this one out. You can always buy one for fun at a future date to try and 'lose' some of your awesome profits! I must admit I love my Teflon-coated super de-luxe American oval cutter, but it doesn't make me any money. But there is a simple handheld oval cutter costing a fraction of the above machine which with practise produces perfect ovals. It has a plastic base with a metal arm that holds the blade. You hold the plastic base down and the arm is pushed round in an oval, producing the bevelled mount – it works for me!

5. Card guillotine

The card guillotine is the traditional 1.22m- (4ft-)long bench end guillotine, a long scimitar blade with a guard and self sharpening edge. They are wonderful for rapidly and accurately cutting backing board, mount board, trimming pictures - all round a most useful if expensive piece of equipment. Nevertheless I would strongly recommend one. The alternative is cutting using a Kraft knife and straight edge. Make sure it has a finger guard. In comparison to the bench end guillotine, it is slow, tedious and dangerous! The mount-cutting machines normally have a built-in method of cutting the mount board to size, usually an arm off the mount cutter with a vertical 'Stanley' type blade on the sliding block. This works well but still leaves you with the problem of cutting your backing board.

6. Vertical cutter

There are several makes of machine designed to cut vertically. These have different cutter heads for card, board and glass respectively, and are designed for those with limited space. In essence they are a wall-mounted frame, into which your material is placed and cut using a block running on a bar placed over the material. I have never used one of these machines, but those who do swear by them. It could help you considerably If you are very short of space.

I would suggest in the case of this machine that you ask the suppliers for a demonstration. Try it for yourself before making the decision to buy. This in fact applies to any machine you decide to buy: get the supplier to demonstrate and have a go yourself.

There you have the main tools of your framing workshop, representing the greatest financial outlay of the business. My feeling has always been that if you have the very best tools and look after them well they will make money for you. They last for years and, although expensive, really do represent value for money. Some years back I completely re-equipped my workshop. I sold off all the main tools without any problem. They had all seen 20 years' service, and yet I sold them all to eager buyers for more than I paid for them new.

There is one other large piece of equipment I would not be without, and that is an upright, powerful cylinder or drum vacuum cleaner – the type that DIY stores sell with easily obtainable filters and spares. This is for cleaning the workshop, but most importantly it is set up under your assembly bench with the flexible tube and a soft brush mounted on the end, enabling every frame to be vacuumed to prevent dust particles, hairs and splinters of glass being left behind the glass. Using a vacuum thus, I have never had any problems. You would not believe the number of framers I have heard moaning about repeatedly having to undo frames to remove flecks of this, that or the other – so get a powerful vacuum cleaner!

There remain the various hand tools you will require:

1. Framing guns – dart guns and staplers. I use a standard stationery stapler with 6mm and 8mm staples.(Beware staplers for DIY as they are designed for fixing board, carpet and other heavy duty applications and will probably be too heavy/powerful for normal framing applications!)

2. For pinning the backs of frames, I use a purpose-designed framer's gun that manually fires flexible darts into the moulding to close the back of the frame. These also come in electric and pneumatic models.

3. Several Stanley-type knives, all with fresh blades. Keep sharp blades to prevent damaging whatever it is you may have to cut. I use scalpels with throwaway blades for fine work. These can be obtained from art shops.

4. Bradawl for boring start holes and an electric rechargeable screwdriver with socket attachments that grip screw eyes to turn them into the frame as well as screw on other fittings.

5. Pliers, blunt and pointed, plus wire clippers, several good pairs of scissors and canvas pliers.

6. Screwdrivers, flat and Pozidriv/Phillips.

7. A couple of hammers, including a square framer's hammer.

8. A good glass cutter for 2mm glass, a set square, straight edge and plastic-cutting Stanley-knife blades.

9. There are various other tools and aids for specific jobs, none of which are expensive. I will describe them individually as they are needed during the various stages of framing.

With the above, you should have a framing workshop that can tackle almost anything, but in saying this I am assuming that you already have basic DIY tools (power drill, jigsaw, etc.), which you might also need from time to time.

A word of warning: whatever tool you are using, do not under any circumstances remove the safety guard – I leave safety guards well alone and I still get perfect results. Don't listen to framers who tell you they don't need the safety guards. Not only is it illegal, it is highly dangerous. Always remember that making picture frames without fingers is well-nigh impossible!

Stocking the Workshop

When stocking your workshop, you will find your suppliers listed in the various directories in your local library, which is a wonderful reference source for whatever you want to do. The other source of information these days is of course the Internet. It often helps to have a supplier near you for emergencies. However, the distant suppliers have no problem dispatching goods to you, and decent-sized orders (within the UK) usually come postage paid.

While stocking your workshop can now be done through a single wholesaler, I personally prefer to keep accounts with several to ensure that at the very least I have back-up supplies. Particularly in the early stages of developing your business, it is important to buy only the minimum stock you require for the orders you expect to receive. As the client base grows, you can increase your stock. Compare this to setting up as an artist, where the artist has to produce the work, frame it, leave it in a gallery on sale or return, where the frame will possibly be damaged (expense borne by the artist) and where, if it is sold, there may be the further problem of extracting money from the gallery owner! With framing, be it trade or bespoke, you possess the framed pictures, so 'no pay, no frames'. Bad debts have never been a problem, especially when compared to the artist's world or to any other business, for that matter, where the producer relies on other people to stock and sell their product!

The following is a list of the various items of stock and the materials you will need:

1. Moulding

As already mentioned, picture-frame moulding comes in 2- or 3-metre lengths and is made in a mind-boggling array of patterns, colours and finishes. It is normally wood-based, with various finishes, but there are also plastic and metal mouldings. The plastic handles much like wood does; the metal, if pure alloy, requires special cutting, often using mitre saws.

I personally avoid plastic and metal although I do stock the metal-covered moulding, which is a wooden moulding with a soft alloy covering in various finishes from bright to matt, silver to gold. They play havoc with mitre blades, so I always charge extra and spend a few moments crying into my beer before thinking of the profit puts a smile back on my face!

Moulding is supplied in 30-metre batches, although most suppliers will happily provide 15-metre batches, and often less, though for the most part they will charge more pro rata! To start with, 15 metres is the ideal amount of each moulding to have. Suppliers also provide samples – 15cm-long (6 in.) pieces of the various mouldings they stock.

When starting, it is probably best to buy between 10 and 12 of the most commonly used mouldings. To help the customer choose which moulding they prefer, it is a good idea to make up right angles, i.e. two pieces of moulding 8 in long fixed at the mitre. You should be able to persuade the supplier to let you have another dozen or so samples to make up a decent sample display.

Your mouldings will range from the narrow 15mm (½in) pieces to big expensive ones 100mm (4in.) wide; but you will rarely sell these larger mouldings, so it is best to buy these only as and when you need them. Your wholesaler will have a representative who will prove very useful in helping you decide on your initial stock. Keep it simple to start with and get a nice sober range from the small simple black-cushion moulding through light and dark wood to silver and gilt, which in turn ranges from bright to antique, plus some colour-finished mouldings.

You can gradually increase your stock to include some 35 to 40 mouldings, bearing in mind that if you are trade framing for local shops you must always keep in stock the range displayed in the shops: you will not be popular if you are constantly telling the shopkeeper (who in turn has to tell his customer) that the order cannot be fulfilled or else will be late. If you mess around with your customers, they tend not to return! This of course applies to mount board as well. Remember, when starting your business, not to overstock or overspend on moulding – you will soon get a feel for what sells and in what quantity.

It is best to store your moulding in racks along the wall behind the guillotine, where it is out of the way but easily accessed, or on cross-beams at ceiling height if there is headroom. Storing the moulding high up keeps it away from moist air at lower levels. Remember to pad the racking, and stack it carefully: it is prone to warping and can be expensive to lose.

2. Mount board

Mount board is now normally sold by the framing wholesaler and comes in a vast range of colours, textures and thicknesses. It is now usually neutral or acid-free, thus preventing your framing masterpiece from turning its cherished picture yellow! There is also far more expensive museum-quality mount board which, as the name implies, is for the preservation of artworks, but I use the standard acid-free, bleached virgin wood-fibre that is lignin-free (a board that is buffered with calcium carbonate).

Double Imperial 1120 x 815mm (44 x 32in.) is the standard sheet size (buying the largest is the most economical). Once again, you need to start with a range of 15 to 20 different colours. Don't worry too much about the huge range of textured and patterned boards. A range of cream, white, pastel and dark shades will start you off. I have at times been given manufacturers' sample blocks containing beautifully cut samples of their entire range – once again useful for the customer who wants something different and is happy to wait till you get in his special order! In practice I find that I need relatively few board varieties, and only a few patterned boards.

Your stacking system for the boards should be under the mount-cutting bench in the 30cm-wide (1ft) sections. The board is packed in vertical, on edge, and I keep the sections tight by inserting a sheet of plywood the same size as the boards and locking it in place. I carry 10 sheets of every colour, but some of the suppliers do multicolour packs of 5 or 10 sheets that can help get you started. Remember that a customer will often come in with a set of prints or pictures that requires a set of mounts, so keep enough in stock for half a dozen identical mounts, i.e. usually five sheets.

3. Backing board

For many years, backing board was made of card strawboard; then 2mm hardboard came into fashion and more recently MDF (medium-density fibreboard). Both hardboard and MDF are still available.

There are health fears with these materials: framers cut them using power saws, which creates noxious dust, so remember to wear a mask if you are doing this. I find that both boards cut easily and cleanly on the bench-end guillotine, thus avoiding the problem of dust. There is also grey pulp board in several thicknesses, which is worth stocking for all sorts of backing jobs. Finally, there are the new foam-core boards, comprised of polystyrene foam between two smooth outer layers usually made of paper. This is much more expensive than hardboard or MDF, but it has its advantages: it is very light, easily cut and can be used in a variety of ways to make box frames or shadow boxes (see 'Moulding' on page 81).

You will probably eventually need to stock all the different backing boards to have the variety to match a wide range of frames, but hardboard/MDF is the backing I use in vast quantities, probably 10 times more than any others. Start with sufficient stock for about 20 frames, i.e. 10 sheets of each.

4. Glass

Glass for the most part is not supplied by the moulding wholesalers. There are various firms scattered around the country who supply A-grade float glass to framers. It comes in 90cm x 150cm (3 x 5 ft) sheets, of which you normally buy 25 at a time. Do not go to your local glazier as he will charge you a fortune! Look up 'Glass Wholesalers' in the trade directories at your local library.

The second variety of glass you should stock is non-reflecting glass. This comes in larger sheets, normally 1.8m x 1.2m (6ft x 4ft), but the supplier always cuts them in half for me prior to delivery. I usually keep 10 sheets in stock, although these days I rarely use them.

The third variety of glazing is plastic glass – styrene clear plastic glass sheets, either clear or non-glare, protected on both sides by a layer of polythene. They are UV-stabilised and are cut with a special blade which scores the plastic. You then snap it off over the edge of the bench. Its one great drawback is a maddening tendency to collect dust by way of a static electrical charge. I only use it if specifically requested to or if I am framing one of those long school or college photos that have been taken on a rotating camera – the sort of photo that is 1.2m x 15cm (4ft x 6in.): the flexing would probably break 2mm glass. Fortunately, these seem no longer to be fashionable, as I have not had a long school photo to frame in years.

There is also a new UV-filtering glass that is worth stocking for pictures that need special protection.

5. Sundries

This is the final heading for the major stock section and includes those various fixings and fittings classed as frame furniture. As a rough guide you will need to have:

1. Pins, nails, staples, wedges and blades for your guns and cutters – supplied by the wholesaler who supplied the tools.

2. Picture-hanging furniture, namely screw eyes, rings, D-rings, mirror-plates and several other patent hangings, plus the picture string (non-stretch or picture wire). I carry three thicknesses of the steel-cored brass wire for hangings – I never use string (I had an early accident: a very irate customer came back with a broken frame. She had hung it up, stood back to admire it and it had fallen with a seismic crash at her feet when the string had come adrift. I have avoided string ever since and have never had a repeat of that very embarrassing incident.) You will also have turn buttons, strut backs and clip springs for supporting photo frames. There are numerous products to aid framers, from canvas fixings to frameless glass clips, but if you start with a good pinning system, a hanging system, and mirror plates and turn buttons, you can add others as you grow. I also carry brass picture hooks and pins as I always give a free wall hanging with every frame – it's a nice touch and is always appreciated.

3. Tapes. I use 4cm, 5cm and 7.5cm (1in., 2in. and 3in.) brown gummed paper tape for finishing the backs. (I have explained why under 'Finishing the Frame' in Hobby/Small-scale Framing.) I keep my tapes on homemade rollers under the shelf in front of the finishing table along with rolls of 2.5cm and 5cm (1in. and 2in.) masking tape, Sellotape, and brown vinyl tape on a gun dispenser for parcelling up frames. Finally, you will need a very good quality double-sided tape for hanging pictures behind mounts. Make sure it will not damage the pictures. I use conservation-quality tapes for this purpose .

4. Copydex is a useful glue to keep in the workshop and for gluing moulding I use resin PVA wood glue, which is non-toxic, safe and strong.

5. I also carry a 90cm roll of Kraft paper and a roll of bubble wrap to protect completed framing jobs. Remember that presentation is important: if you deliver your customers' expensive frames in old waste paper, like second-rate fish and chips, you probably won't see them again!

MAKING PICTURE FRAMES
Categories of Picture Frames

You will find the frames you make fall into basic categories as follows:
1. Frames only
2. Frames with glazing
3. Frames with mounts (matts) and glazing
4. Frames for tapestries/embroideries.

Occasionally you will get a frame that does not fit into these categories, e.g. for coins, medals or three-dimensional objects – these are dealt with on page 94.

1. Frames only

This is the framing for oil paintings or acrylics that are either on a board or canvas and do not require glazing. You may also get notice-boards, maps, diagrams, etc. to frame, which the customer for one reason or another does not want glazed.

2. Frames with glazing

These are objects or pictures to be framed behind glass. They are known as 'close frames' and can include certificates, pictures, photographs, etc. Whenever you 'close-frame' a picture, remember to leave a space between the end of the rebate and the paper to allow for expansion and contraction of the picture in response to changes in atmospheric conditions.

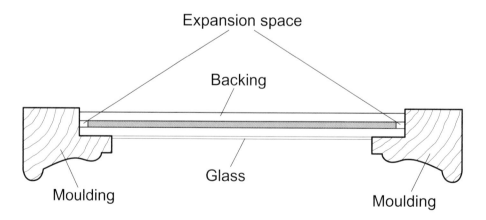

Allow for picture expansion

If a picture is 'tightly' framed, when it expands due to a change of atmosphere it will 'cockle'. When you look at framed pictures you will often notice that they sometimes have wavelike ripples on the surface. These look unsightly and are caused by framers 'cramming' the picture into the frame so that when it expands it cockles. In fact, once you have an interest in framing, you will find yourself constantly studying frames – in friends' homes, galleries, shops. It can become a bit of an obsession, a sort of 'spot the mistake' – you will be amazed at the botched jobs you see! Don't go round loudly pointing out the faults or you may find your circle of friends rapidly diminishing! The habit is, however, very good for your own quality control.

3. Frames with mounts (matts)

A mount, or a 'matt' as it is called in the USA, is a coloured, sometimes textured card surround that is placed behind the glass and before the picture. It has an aperture cut out to reveal the picture, the inside edge of the aperture being made with a 45-degree bevelled cut that reveals a pleasing white border between mount and picture.

The picture is hung behind the mount with a fixing along its top edge; the other three edges remain free in order to let the picture expand and contract naturally. The other good reason for a mount, apart from the aesthetic appeal of enhancing the picture, is to keep the picture off the glass. Glass is very susceptible to temperature change and a space protects the picture from such fluctuations.

4. Frames for tapestries, embroideries and cross stitches

There is a fourth category of framing service you can offer which many framers do not. Thus framing tapestries, embroideries and cross stitches can be lucrative work. The artwork is 'stretched' over either a frame or a board and fixed in place, usually sewn - glue should not be used in such circumstances. Recently I was brought in an exquisite piece of work: a cockerel embroidered onto a panel. Its creator had spent many hours quite literally embroidering in every feather. The effect was absolutely stunning. You can imagine my horror when I discovered that the previous framer (an alleged professional, I've still got his label and address on the workshop wall – I stick pins in it from time to time!) had glued the mount to the front of the artwork and glued the artwork itself to the backing board. The only thing I could do was to spend an entire day carefully unpicking the piece and cleaning off the glue. I stitched it onto a piece of museum board and then framed it. It looked great. Under the circumstances I did not charge the customer the full cost of my time, but I do strongly suggest you avoid glue!

Making The Frame

1. Job sheet

You will need a job sheet when making your frames. I always use an offcut of mount board on which I write all the measurements and calculations: moulding number and type, mount board number and colour, type of glass, type of picture (the pictures are kept in their secure store until they are ready for assembly in the frame). The idea is to minimise the chance of mistakes and accidents. Make it a rule to prepare a job sheet whether you have one or 100 pictures to frame. Also, to avoid mistaking one dimension for another, always use the same sequence on the job sheet. Keep the dated job sheets in a box so that you can always refer back from order to job sheet to invoice.

Order No.	Picture	Picture Size	Mountboard		Frame size/ Backing	Glass	Notes
			Colour	Width			
123	OIL ON CANVAS	20" x 30"			20 x 30		FRAME ONLY
224	PHOTO	10" x 8"	BLACK	2"	14" x 12"	O/R	
225	W/COLOUR	16 x 12	CREAM	3"	22 x 18	O/R	GREEN WASHLINE

Job sheet

You should always endeavour to keep your customers' pictures secure and limit your handling of them. When writing up your job sheet measure and note down all relevant details of the picture, then store it in a secure place. You will need it again only when the frame is finished and the picture can be inserted. Do not leave customers' property 'floating' around the workshop – the risk of accidental damage is too great!

2. Moulding

Take out the length of moulding to be cut, unwrap it carefully and examine it closely for flaws on the face, checking for damage, warps or twists. If the length is bad I always keep it to one side, notifying the suppliers and showing the length to the representative when he calls.

Moulding is packed in individual lengths, pairs or multiples at the factory, and you will occasionally find when you unwrap them that lengths twist or bend. It happens, and it's Murphy's Law that you will always have a problem with the last length and a very impatient customer.

When moulding is manufactured, the wood is first milled to the required profile. This is done with two lengths simultaneously. They are joined like Siamese twins along the rebate and are subsequently split before the final finish is applied. With ornate or decorated frames this finish will be a 'compo' layer, also called 'gesso' (originally gypsum or chalk or plaster of Paris but more recently a plastic mixture) applied to the face of the wood. A metal roller with the pattern cut into the surface is then passed over the gesso, imprinting the pattern on the frame. This is usually applied to left and right mouldings before they are split. It is very important to remember that the left and right hand will not marry up, so your moulding must be from the same batch and the same side to give you a perfect frame. (Moulding is usually marked L or R on the rear of the length!) Offcuts or remnants that do not match are best kept in your offcut box for a smaller frame where offcuts can be used. Do not try and make frames with lengths from different batches. They will not work.

Having checked your moulding, you can cut the individual pieces on the guillotine. This is a simple operation that entails setting the stop measurement, trimming the end of the moulding, sliding it to the stop, setting the rebate supports and using multiple cuts to 'nibble' through the moulding to achieve two perfect mitres. Remove the cut piece, slide the length on and cut another piece. Now move the stop to the second measurement and repeat the process for the final two lengths. In cutting, it is important not to cause any damage to the face of the moulding either on the length or at the cut. Never make a frame then try to make good a bad mitre. Your guillotine is a precision tool that, properly set up, will give you a mitre joint so fine as to be virtually invisible. Anything less than perfect and you should recut the frame. The reject pieces can have the flaws and damaged parts cut out ready to be used on frames of different dimensions. Having cut the frame, check under the rebate. You may find that some bits of wood splinter on the underside of the rebate. Trim them off to prevent them getting into the joint.

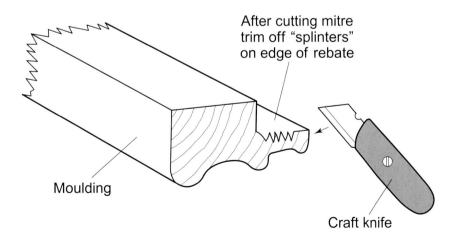

Trim splinters

When cutting the frame, it is essential that the moulding is absolutely flat on the guillotine top so that the blade cuts at exactly 90 degrees to the moulding. If the moulding is not held flat, you will find that your frame does not lie flat. An exact 45-degree mitre is needed to join the frame perfectly together; the mitres must fit precisely face to face.

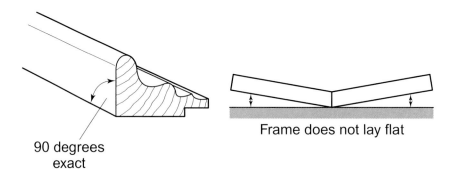

90 degrees
exact

Frame does not lay flat

If the frame does not lie flat, your moulding was either warped or you did not have the moulding flat on the guillotine table.

3. Assembling your frame

Having cut your frame, it is time to assemble it. (See Section One for cutting by hand. Here my primary object is to produce professional-quality frames, which you will never achieve using hand-saws, mitre blocks and shooting blocks.) The traditional and still often-used method is clamping and pinning, but over the last 20 years the underpinner has become the main means of fixing. I use both the underpinner and the framer's vice and pins.

With a framer's vice, place a length and width into the vice and adjust them to make a perfect fit. Having done so, remove one piece, cover the mitre with a thin layer of glue and return to the vice. Then pre-drill a pair of holes and insert the panel pins. Tap them down and, using a centre punch, countersink them below the surface. Remove from the vice and set aside, repeating the operation with the second pair of lengths or 'L's. Always pin in the same direction and always put the length and one width on the same side. This will ensure you get a frame whose halves ('L's) marry up and are both pinned in either a clockwise or an anticlockwise direction. Leave the 'L's overnight to enable the glue to dry completely. A good framer's vice holds the two glued pieces of moulding together with sufficient pressure to ensure they form a very strong mitre joint when pinned. (See page 45 for illustration of Framer's Vice).

MAKING FRAME (PROFESSIONAL)

1. Guillotine trims off moulding length to obtain first mitre cut. Note rebate supports set under rebate on left hand side of moulding.

2. Guillotine trims (nibbles) through moulding in several cuts.

3. Set the callibrated scale for the length/width of frame.

4. Cut length to size.

5. Nibble cuts protect guillotine/moulding from excessive force.

6 Setting the underpinners top pressure pad which holds the moulding in place while pinning. (Note: this underpinner is a pneumatic model.)

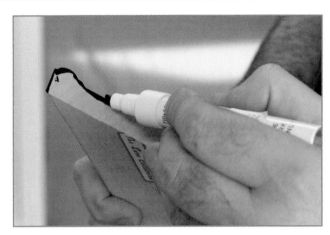

7. Mark top edge of mitre with indelible black felt pen to ensure that no light wood shows on the dark moulding face (useful tip!)

8. Hold moulding length in underpinner, lower pressure pad and insert wedge.

9. Shows the wedged and glued mitre – the process is repeated for all corners.

To underpin your frame, take the length and width of the moulding and place them on the table of the underpinner. Adjust the backstop to position your wedge where you want it, then adjust the pressure pad above to hold the moulding without crushing the face. Glue and insert the wedge, or wedges, if required. Once again, I tend to make the 'L's and leave them to dry overnight before completing the frame.

As I said earlier, I am not convinced as to the strength of the glue joints using the underpinner, so with any frame larger than A4 size (as a rough guide), I tend to clamp the frame. For this purpose I normally use the Stanley plastic picture clamps, or the Ulmia clamps for larger moulding. Having clamped the frame, I then set the underpinner and wedge the joints.

You then have a complete frame, pinned (wedged), glued and clamped under pressure. Leave it overnight for the glue to dry. Remember that with white PVA resin glue, once dried under pressure, the joint will be stronger than the wood! In the latest underpinners the pressure problem is dealt with by toothed clamps that pull the moulding in so that the corner is automatically held and pinned under pressure. At all times, remember to protect the face of your moulding, taking care to prevent glue coming through the joint to deface it. I always keep cheap rolls of toilet paper scattered around the workshop for wiping away glue, etc.

DETAIL OF FIXINGS – UNDERPINNER WEDGES

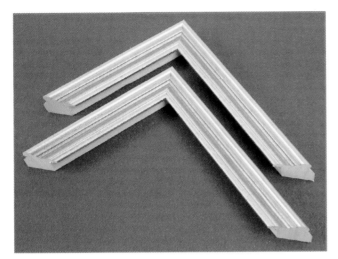

1. Shows 'L's of moulding pinned and glued – it is often better to leave these to dry overnight before making up the final two joints.

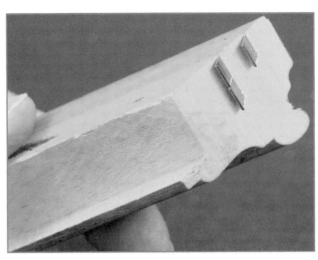

2. Shows wedges in the moulding inserted from below – they can be 'stacked', i.e. one punched in after another to increase the depth of the joint. Each wedge is a 'V' shape with two small flanges; one side has a 'bladed' edge for penetration into the wood.

3. Side view of wedges.

4. Shows 3 wedges in the mitre joint from below.

5. The completed frame.

MACHINE CUTTING A MOUNT

1. The mount cutting machine has the built in facility to trim the outer dimensions of the mount board very accurately.

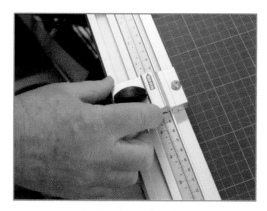

2. Set the calibration.

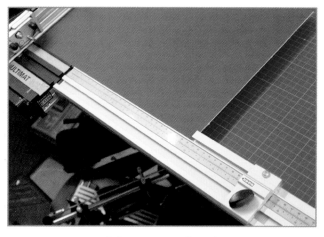

3. Insert mount board.

4. Trim to size.

5. Place under slide after setting calibration cut.

6. Shows the cutter head on its sliding bar which lies onto the rear of the mountboard.

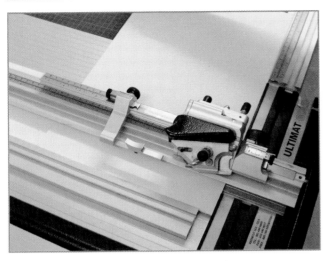

7. Turn the mount board.

8. Cut.

9. Partially cut mount.

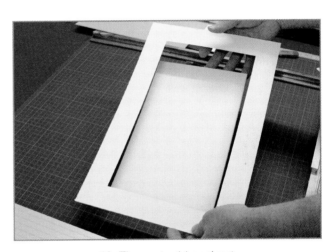

10. The centre 'drops' out.

11. The mount cut and ready for use.

4. Stacking

You should have numerous padded under-bench shelves for stacking work in progress. If you put a frame down on the padded surface, you will normally be able to stack anything up to five frames on top, though always face down and at right angles to one another.

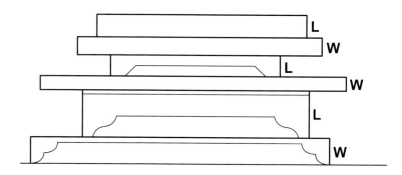

When stacking frames, place face down and alternate length and width. Never slide frames.

Remember to place them down gently. If you slide them, you risk scratching and damaging them. If you are worried about damage, keep a number of pieces of soft card that can be used as dividers.

5. Mounts

Having made your frames and stacked them to allow the glue to dry, turn your attention to the next process, which is the mount-cutting. Firstly, work out the width of your mount. You will normally do this when you are measuring the picture to write up your job sheet. Modern mount-cutting machines work best when you have mounts of even width all round. The traditional style of mount was to have a bottom margin significantly wider than the other three sides. I don't think it is necessary, but it does work on some pictures. To obtain this effect on machine-cut mounts, make all sides the same width as the bottom then trim the sides and top down to the desired proportions.

The width of the mount is basically determined by the width you think best enhances the picture. The type of mount used will also determine the dimensions – for instance, double mount, triple mount, wash-line mount. The varieties of mount will be dealt with later, but for the moment we are concentrating on the basic cutting.

With a mount-cutting machine, you cut your card to the mount/cards outer dimension either with a Stanley knife or guillotine or with the built-in cutter on the mount-cutting machine. This outer cut *must be accurate*, as the accuracy of the aperture depends on the outer cut. Once you have your outer measurement, you set the mount-cutting machine to the desired width and length of cut and, depending on the type of machine, cut the two opposite sides or cut in sequence to produce the aperture. These machines cut from the back of the card and work on the principle of a blade in a sliding running block on a bar that can be lowered onto the moulding. Beware of unnecessary and very unsightly overcuts on the corners!

The other method is hand-cutting with various patent cutters and knives. This is fine if you are doing only a few mounts per week, but machine-cutting will reduce the time needed to cut each mount to two or three minutes.

Always store the offcuts carefully, as these will provide material for the mounts for smaller pictures. However, try to minimise waste by pre-planning how to cut your larger sheets of card. Having cut your mounts, put them to one side and move on to the next stage, which is glass-cutting.

6. Glass-cutting

I use a specific 2mm glass cutter with a tungsten-carbide wheel, which I keep dipped in a little jar containing 50% oil and 50% pure turpentine. (I actually use extra virgin olive oil from the kitchen: it keeps the cutter wheel in very good condition!)

Protecting your glass cutter

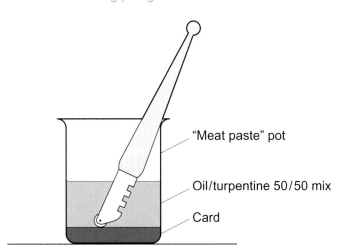

"Meat paste" pot

Oil/turpentine 50/50 mix

Card

To mark the glass, I use extra-fine fibre-tip pens – not the indelible type, but ones that will give sufficient marking to be clearly visible and can also be wiped off easily!

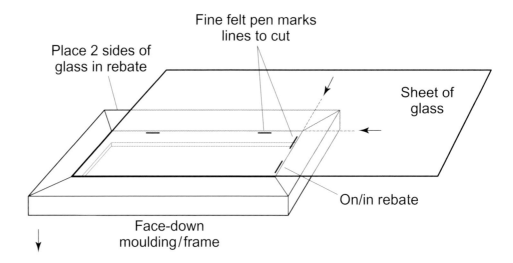

Marking glass for cutting

When starting with a complete sheet of glass, I usually rough-cut it to the approximate width of the frame. Do this for the whole sheet so that your pieces are more manageable, then carefully place the glass over the frame so that two sides of the glass fit into the length and width rebate of the frame. Mark the glass along the line of the other two sides. Remove the frame and, with your square, cut the glass along the marks. Remove the surplus and cut the remaining side. Brush the glass to remove fine splinters and drop it into the frame. It should fit snugly – though not too tight – so that you can lift it out without effort. A 2.5 mm gap between the glass and the end of the rebate is ideal.

Cutting glass is very easy, but you must be confident. Place your guide on the glass and run the cutter along the glass to produce a single line. If you get the pressure right, the cutter literally sings as it runs, leaving a fine line. NEVER GO BACK OVER THE LINE: it is a one-movement operation. Lift the edge of the glass where the line ends. Place the ball end of the cutter under the line and with a short sharp pressure break the glass along the line (I put two fingers of one hand on the left-hand side and with the fingers of the right hand give a sharp push to the right). With practice, the glass will break cleanly along the line – though not always! A pair of glass pliers will trim off any excess. With practice you will break perfectly 99% of the time!

Breaking scored glass

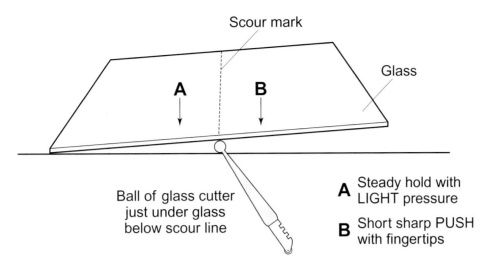

Scour mark

Glass

A

B

Ball of glass cutter
just under glass
below scour line

A Steady hold with
LIGHT pressure

B Short sharp PUSH
with fingertips

With longer cuts on larger pieces, once you have scored the glass move the sheet over until the score is just over the edge of the bench. Then, with a short, sharp (but not excessive) tweak, snap off the cut. Once again, practice will make this a routine job.

Remember when working with glass to observe the following essential safety guidelines:

1. Never slide your hand
2. Always use deliberate movements
3. Wear eye protection
4. Keep other people away from your working area.

It is worth noting at this point that any sliding movements in picture framing should always be avoided. Frames get scratched, so does glass. Always pick up and put down deliberately. Train yourself to do it. In fact, this is the most important safety rule: *always use* deliberate movements. Never, never slide!

Between each cut, brush the cutting table to minimise splinters – they scratch and damage subsequent sheets of glass! Use a fairly hard brush, the type that is usually sold with a plastic dustpan.

Finally, there are several frameless systems which entail clipping the glass, backing and picture together in a sandwich. They were originally invented to help people bypass the cost of framing. The chances are you will never need them, but if you do it will be necessary to de-edge your glass. To do this is very simple: cut the glass and then, placing the edge of the glass on the end of the bench, take off the sharp portion by rubbing gently with a small oilstone until it is rounded and safe.

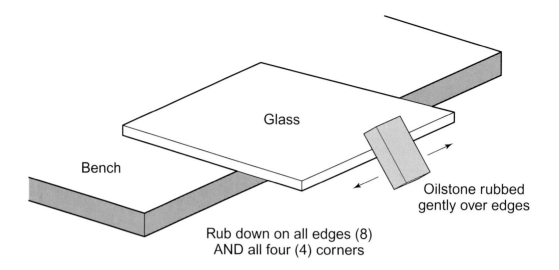

De-edging the glass

Repeat the process for all eight sharp edges on the sheet and give the corners a rub at the end. This produces a 'safe' piece of glass, though of course no piece of glass is ever safe.

7. Backing board

The final piece of the framing jigsaw is the backing board, which is cut to fit the rear of the frame. Once again, this should be a loose fit to allow for expansion and contraction. Cut the board on the guillotine (if you have one, or if not with a Kraft knife) and, using the glass in the frame to act as a template, mark your board with a pencil prior to cutting. Remember to plan your cuts so as to minimise waste, and store your offcuts for use on smaller frames.

You have now made your frame, pinned and glued its joints, and cut the glass, backing and mount. It is time for the final phase – assembly and finishing.

CUTTING GLASS

Offer glass up to frame and mark the two edges for cutting with fine felt pen.

Place rule on glass and run cutter over the glass (once only – make it sing!)

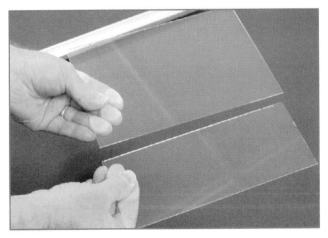

With a positive action, snap along line, like this on a small piece or on the bench edge or with the 'ball' on the end of the glass cutter wheel.

Assembling the Frame

You now have the component parts of your picture frame made and ready for assembly.

Firstly, clean the glass on both sides. Cleaning the glass requires a very good glass cleaner. I use a dedicated cleaner called Nilglass which my wholesaler sells. It does not leave smears. I have two dusters (well worn, without excess fluff), one to apply the cleaner and the other to polish.

Clean both sides and then hold up to the light to check for missed areas or other marks. Good glass cleaning is absolutely vital and to this end you should endeavour to wash your cleaning cloths frequently. Once you are satisfied that your glass is clean, put the backing board into the frame to protect the glass.

It is at this point that I should mention the tide marks that occasionally appear on glass when wet. These are ripples of pattern that appear in the surface that left me mystified for many years and drew blank stares from glass suppliers. I eventually found the cause. When the glass is delivered, it is often separated by sheets of paper, like thin newsprint, to protect the glass. If left between the glass, this paper absorbs moisture, and the acid in the paper etches the surface of the glass. It was very annoying, but after I pointed it out to my supplier it became a problem of the past. I have nonetheless noticed the paper between the glass at other glaziers' and framers' premises; it is best removed when the glass is delivered.

Having cleaned the glass, it is time to prepare the mount. Make sure it fits the frame snugly (don't forget to leave room for expansion and contraction), and if required put double mounts together.

You are now ready to take the picture out of storage and put it into the frame. I tend to put all the pictures in place ready for the final assembly; in other words, trim, fit them in mounts and put backing on the pictures where necessary.

To assemble, start with the frame in front of you. Lift out the backing, so you are left with the moulding frame and the glass. Switch on the vacuum, which ideally will plug into the front of the bench with an easy-access switch. On the long hose, using a clean circular brush head that is kept specifically for this purpose, brush and dust the glass and the inside of the rebate. Dust the front of the picture and the mount, and carefully place them in the frame. Then dust the backing board and place it on top. Run the brush round the slight gap between contents and moulding, replace the brush and switch off the vacuum cleaner. Put the frame against the stop bar and put two pins in on each side, near the mitre.

Carefully lift up the frame and make sure that there are no dust flecks trapped under the glass and that the mount and picture both sit straight. I use an old set of dividers (out of a geometry set) to make sure everything is even. If all is well, replace the frame on the bench and complete the pinning of the back. I place my darts or pins at about 10cm (4in.) intervals. Turn the frame over and check for damage, inaccuracies and dust. Be very critical – you should want perfection! If there is a problem, you can put it right at this stage, before you start taping up. Repeat the process with all the frames you are making.

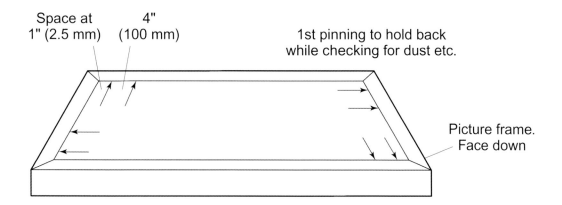

Space at 1" (2.5 mm) 4" (100 mm) 1st pinning to hold back while checking for dust etc.

Picture frame. Face down

Making good

There will often be production marks on the spine of the moulding at the mitres. These will be clamp marks and countersunk panel pinholes, and occasionally chips in the moulding caused by the downward pressure of the guillotine on the spine.

Remember that there should be no damage to the face of the moulding. If there is, reject the entire frame and recut. You can never match up, and in the long run it is cheaper and better for your reputation to have a perfect frame. You can always recut and reuse the rejected frame at a later date.

Any production marks should be filled. I use Brummer's Interior Stopping in white or cream, made by Clam-Brummer Ltd. This paste does not shrink, adheres well, any excess can be wiped off with a damp cloth, it can be fine-sanded and it takes colour well. I then cover this with wax gilt matched to the moulding finish, or if it is coloured I use artists' acrylic mixed in very small amounts and matched to the frame colour – but remember, too little rather than too much! I mix the acrylics on glass offcuts and with care I can always get a perfect match.

Taping up

Taping up is the sealing of the rear of the frame to prevent dust entering. There are many makes of pre-gummed sticky tape on the market, usually of a plastic nature. (I've even seen brown plastic packaging tape used!) I would only recommend one method, and that is the traditional brown paper tape, or gum-strip tape, which is pre-glued and requires wetting to stick it to the frame. Gum-strip can be completely and cleanly removed (even years on) by simply wetting the tape, waiting for the glue to soften and peeling it off. Any glue on the moulding wipes off with a damp cloth.

I carry 4cm, 5cm and 7.5cm-wide (1.5in., 2in. and 3in.) rolls on dispensers fixed under the shelf. These pull out and can be cut to size, 8mm (¼in.) shorter than the frame. They are then placed on a hardboard offcut approximately 1m x 20cm (3ft 3in. x 8in.) and wetted with water using a 5cm (2in.) decorator's brush in a dog's plastic water bowl (non-spill). First place the tape along the two short sides of the frame, then along the long sides. Position carefully, wipe smooth and leave to dry overnight.

Some framers do fiddly mitre cuts at the corners – frankly, if you place the tape neatly, it is a waste of time. The only real variation you will find to the preceding assembly system is when making open glassless frames, such as those for oils on canvas. In these cases I like first to line the back of the moulding and rebate with gum-strip paper. Once it has dried, I put the canvas with its stretcher into the rebate and fix in place using one of the patent systems, or by tapping in a panel pin at an angle and bending it over the back of the canvas to hold it in place. These pins can then be twisted aside to take out the canvas. (Take care over how deep you insert the pins – don't go right through the face of the moulding!)

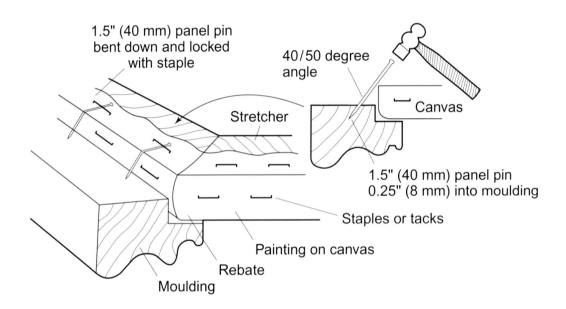

Before bending the pin over, place a piece of tape on the canvas (to protect the canvas from rust should the pin corrode) and then put a couple of easily removed wire staples across the pin to lock it in place. I always cover the back of the canvas with a thin card panel taped to the moulding to offer the rear of the picture protection from dust, etc.

Finally, you will frequently get pictures to frame that have dedications or information labels, or else pictures to reframe that have valuable information on the original frame. Rather than simply sticking this onto the backing, I always cut and clean an offcut of glass that adequately covers the relevant information. I then place this on the backing board and fix it in place with gum-strip paper when I am taping up the back of the picture. This is always well received by the customer!

Fixing, hangings and frame furniture

The final process of assembly is the fitting of the furniture, which means the hangings.

Hanging furniture is either eyes, rings on eyes or D-rings in the moulding. Other hangings can be riveted onto the backing board. A rule of thumb is that hangings are fixed one third of the distance from the top of the frame. You then have the choice of non-stretch cord or wire. I use multi-strand brass wire with a steel core in one of three sizes, between screwed-in D-rings. Once again, appearance is important, so tie the cord neatly, or in the case of wire twist it neatly up to the ring. A bit of practice and you should have a neat finish (a bit like a hangman's noose or a whipped rope end). Bear in mind that hangings on the back of a frame can cause awful damage to the front of a frame when it is stacked; so if you are bespoke framing for shops or agents, make the holes in the moulding to accept screws or eyes, but don't fix them. Instead place a couple of screw eyes and a length of wire neatly coiled onto the backing, secured with Sellotape. This should reduce the chances of the frame being damaged in the shop. I have a rubber stamp (the simple self-inking type of machine) that said 'PLEASE ENSURE RINGS AND WIRE ARE SECURE BEFORE HANGING', which I stamp on the back of every frame to make sure the customer takes care over hanging.

Finally, wrap your pictures well. Take a large enough sheet of kraft paper off the roll and place it on the bench. Then cut a piece of bubble wrap the same size as the frame, place this on the kraft paper and put the frame face down on top. Fold the paper over and tape up. If I have to stack or load a client's car, I always place the frames in pairs, face to face, back to back, and tell the customer how to look after their frames. You are the expert, and that includes making sure they get their frames home and hung without mishap!

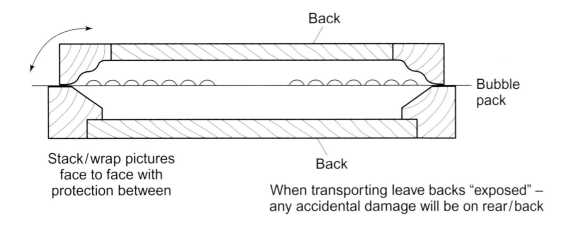

Back

Bubble pack

Stack/wrap pictures
face to face with
protection between

Back

When transporting leave backs "exposed" –
any accidental damage will be on rear/back

SELLING YOURSELF AND YOUR FRAMING

Pricing

The following is the calculation I use to obtain my price charts. The charts are designed to give an accurate quote at the outset. I then fill out an order slip (using order books with triplicate sheets and my address stamped on the top). I write down a detailed description of what has been chosen and add the quote. I give a copy to the customer as proof of my having their picture and the choice made, so there is never any dispute as to who said what. If you are framing for local shops, supply them with an order book, which has a copy for the customer, a copy for themselves and a copy for you. Remember that the more people there are in the chain, the greater the risk of misunderstandings. If it is in writing, you are covered.

Calculating your price

When calculating your picture-frame prices, you will require a price based on a small unit, i.e. a square centimetre (or square inch). Having established a small unit price, you can then multiply it on each frame to reflect the area or length of that individual frame.

The picture-frame cost breaks down into three pricing components:

1. Moulding – linear price
2. Glass/Mount/Backing – square price
3. Sundries – static price.

In other words, the moulding price is calculated on the linear cost of the moulding; glass, mount and backing are calculated on the cost per square metre; and sundries are priced on the quantity of hangings, which tends to be the same for all frames. Or to put it another way, divide the moulding cost by the length, i.e. if you buy 30 metres of moulding at £X, divide the £X by 30 then by 100 to obtain the cost per centimetre run of moulding. As for glass, mount board and backing, take the individual costs of each and divide each figure by the number of sheets. Having calculated the cost of a sheet, measure the sheet to calculate how many square centimetres there are in that sheet, then divide the sheet price by this figure, giving you a price per square centimetre.

The sundries tend to have a basic price throughout, so all you have to do is list the necessary components: pins, glue, fastenings, hangings, glass cleaner, tape, filler. You will use roughly the same amount of each of the above on every frame, so stick to one basic price. For example, if you use 5p of each of the materials just listed, the total would be 35p. Therefore, I would work with a figure of 50p to ensure that all sundry costs are more than adequately covered.

Having calculated the above, you can now work out the unit price. The concept behind this price list is based on the cost of two sides of the picture to be framed, i.e. the length and the width, which will give you a complete price. It is tedious to calculate but once done, will enable you to give your customer an on-the-spot quote that you can be sure will be accurate.

Start with the moulding. Take the minimum size of frame you want to make – I use 15 x 10cm (6in. x 4in.). Add these two figures together then multiply by the centimetre length price of the moulding. Continue adding 1 cm to the length and multiplying by the centimetre length price – i.e.

25cm x Price Y, 26cm x Price Y, 27cm x Price Y – until you reach the maximum picture size you think you will be making. My price list goes up to 2.3m (7ft 6in.). Each moulding in your stock has to be calculated this way, but to make life easier your stock can be grouped into categories based on price. I use Groups A–D, for example, where Group A = 5p, B = 10p, C = 15p, D = 20p.

Mount board is then multiplied on the same principle, i.e. 15 x 10 = 25 sq. cm x 1 sq. cm price

To make this calculation easier, draw up a lined page thus:

Length of 2 sides	Moulding Price	Glass Price	Mount Price	Backing Price	Sundries Price	Total

Note that the above calculation is based on the size of the picture. However, if a mount is required, the size of the frame is increased and you must therefore allow for this (and other extras) by adding on the double width of the mount to cover the additional mount board, backing and glass used. To calculate this figure, measure the picture and decide on the width of the mount and double. For example, a 10 x 20cm picture (a total of 30cm) with a 10cm-wide mount will become 20cm x 30cm, giving a total of 50 to read off against the price list.

Having calculated the above, you have your cost-price list. Now decide your mark-up and add this on, producing an identical design of price list for your retail price. If you are trade framing, produce a third version, which will be your trade-price list. Don't mix them up!

Sample Price List

X2 Sides	Price Band 5p per cm	Price Band 10p per cm	Price Band 15p per cm	Price Band 20p per cm
10	£ 5.02	£ 7.60	£10.19	£12.77
11	£ 5.27	£ 8.12	£10.96	£13.81
12	£ 5.53	£ 8.63	£11.74	£14.84

Having produced your basic price list, calculate a unit price for the other services you provide, e.g. tapestry stretching, embroidery stretching, canvas stretching or decorated mounts. These costs should be added to the reference section along with those for double mounts, non-reflecting glass etc., so that you are able to give an accurate price on the spot. For double or triple mounts add a fixed amount per extra sheet of mount board, and do the same for non-reflecting glass. For a frame-only order, take only the linear price of the frame, add on the cost of sundries then multiply the figure to include your mark-up.

Once you have calculated your price list, you will notice a large differential in the prices between Groups A and D. This is brought about by the far higher prices of the large mouldings. Your profits will therefore jump hugely on the larger moulding, but the extra cost will also deter many customers from using these mouldings.

However, the time taken to make a frame is the same irrespective of the size of the moulding. To take account of this you may wish to adjust your profit percentage on each group. Thus, if you decide on a general mark-up of 100%, Group A (the cheapest) might be marked up 150% and Group D (the most expensive) might be reduced to 75%, to adequately cover your labour costs at the bottom end of the scale and to make the expensive mouldings more attractive at the top.

Also, bear in mind the following three points:

1. When calculating the unit price, include VAT if you are not registered. If you are registered leave it out, as you can claim the VAT back and thus the VAT will be a portion of the normal total framing price.
2. Mark the maximum size for any thickness of frame when doing price lists for agents. If you don't, you will find people ordering 1.8 x 1.2m (6 x 4ft) frames with 15mm (½in.) moulding in an effort to get themselves a bargain!
3. Mark-up is the amount you make on top of the cost of materials. It must include waste, plus all your overheads, and of course your profit.

You must be mindful of the going rate for picture framing. You do not want to overprice as custom will drift to the opposition, while at the same time to undercut too dramatically will undermine the sustainability of your business. To find out the going rate, I usually wander into a framer's out of my area, give them the size of an imaginary picture and ask for a quote. Do this for a variety of frames and you will soon get an idea of what you should charge. Do not worry too much about the ethics of spying, because everyone does it. Keeping an eye on the opposition is fairly normal practice!

An old shopkeeper gave me a couple of tips that I have never forgotten. The first is that as long as you make a penny more than you paid, you have made a profit because profit is what is in the bank, not decorating the walls. The second is never lose a customer. Once a person has decided to visit your shop or gallery, the object is to sell them something. For this you have to watch the customer and apply a degree of psychology. When you give the quote, watch their reaction. If they think it is too much they usually look startled, say they'll think about it and flee to the opposition. Offer them discount and they are usually so pleased that they return. Return or repeat custom is the core of your business.

The framing world divides into two categories: people who have things framed and those that never do! You will find that once you have a satisfied customer they return time after time, and strangely at roughly the same intervals – with me it is every couple of months on average. These people will be your bread and butter, and given the service they expect they will be very loyal. (However, you will always notice a slight variation in trade when a new framer starts up in your area – there are always a few who rush off to try the new opposition!)

Remember when pricing for shops that they need to put on their own mark-up, so you must allow for them to increase the price you charge them by anything from 33% to 50%. For volume trade framing, you will make mere pennies per frame. However, these orders run into hundreds of the same-size frame. It is boring work, but added to the whole is grist to the profits mill. Beware of the individual who comes in with one picture, gets a quote and then demands a substantial discount on the one picture because he says he has dozens or even hundreds more. I always reply that when he brings in the volume framing, he can have the discount.

The clear advantage of picture framing as a business is your fairly safe guarantee of being paid – you are in possession of their frame. However, although 90% of customers pay on collection, some will try and pick up the frame and mutter that you should send them the bill. I never allow the frame to leave until I have been paid. The same applies to trade customers. They have the samples, they take the order, the customer collects the frame and pays them. They have no risk or outlay, so for the framer to demand payment on delivery is quite fair. There are customers who are bad payers: the money is in the post, or they will bring it round and it never arrives, or when they do pay they make you feel that you are taking food from their children's mouths. I do not do business with people who behave in this way, as the profit isn't worth the stress. On the other hand you may get large companies coming to you for frames. They normally have an accounting system of 30, 60 or 90 days before payment, which you have to accept. It is my experience that they are generally good for the money.

Finding Customers

The very best source of custom is word of mouth and recommendation. However, if you have a shop or clearly signed premises, you should also attract some passing trade. If you have only a back-garden workshop, you are going to have to find ways of becoming known. In this regard, I have found advertising in local papers and magazines costs a lot for what are fairly small returns. The most effective publicity in my experience was visiting shops – be they galleries, gift shops, antique shops or cafes – and giving them my business card.

Contact your local post office. They will do leaflet drops with the post, usually a minimum of 5,000 at a time. If there are large businesses in your area, a letter to the managing director introducing yourself and your product can pay dividends. Include a few business cards with the letter. Delivering leaflets in person to these businesses can also generate interest. When I first started, I would visit housing estates or villages and spend a couple of hours pushing nicely produced leaflets or business cards through their letter boxes. Do the same for industrial units.

Also, visit the local art clubs. They often have members who make frames, but you will always find half a dozen or more members who like to be different. Offering the club a substantial discount often helps. Schools, colleges and courses that give out certificates are worth targeting too.

Of course, you won't be able to spend all your time publicising yourself. So set a target, say, two hours per week, to target one area or estate.

THREE

Aspects of Framing

Moulding

The range of mouldings is huge. The normal practice is to buy the moulding ready-made from the wholesaler. You can, however, produce your own by buying milled timber moulding without any finish and decorating and finishing it to your own taste using stains, colours, varnishes and various metallic and gold-leaf finishes.

My tutor, who was of the old school of framers, told me of the skills he had learned during his seven years' apprenticeship under a picture framer. He produced individual frames by making up the frame in a basic wooden moulding. Next he would carve a design into the moulding with chisels, then guild and varnish the frame, applying an antique finish with a final distressing. The end result was a stunningly beautiful and stunningly expensive frame! You do not have to be so lavish. Your best bet is to experiment by buying ready-cut profiles and applying different finishes – artists' acrylic paints can be very effective. (In this regard, see also the separate chapter in this section on gilding.)

Swept frames are mouldings made up into frames. A decorative moulding is then applied to the corners and along the sides, then sections are cut out and pierced to give you the swept-frame effect.

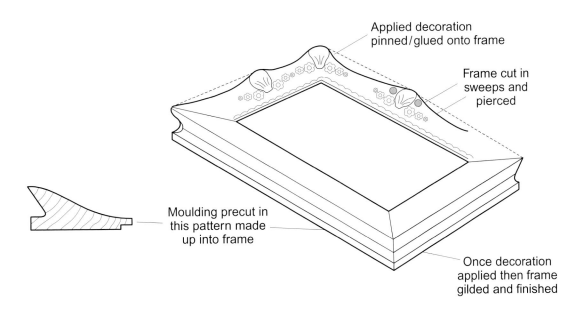

Applied decoration pinned/glued onto frame

Frame cut in sweeps and pierced

Moulding precut in this pattern made up into frame

Once decoration applied then frame gilded and finished

Swept frame

These frames are produced in large quantities in the Far East to standard sizes, and the quality is so good that frankly I do not feel it is worth making them. What I have found rewarding is to individualise frames by gluing designs of my own onto a wooden moulding base. To do this, I use a children's modelling dough which is sculpted or cut to the shape I want, glued to the frame and coated with patent gesso. Gesso is a mixture of rabbit-skin glue and whiting; mercifully, there are now numerous pre-prepared gessoes on the market. The frame is then gilded and finished to produce a very elegant product that is both unique and long-lasting (those I made 25 years ago still look as good as new).

I occasionally play around with individual frames, but my experience is that they are costly to produce, time-consuming and in the UK rarely profitable. If you are framing to make money, stick to the ready-made.

Slip frames

These are flat mouldings cut to fit within the rebate of the outer frame, either to widen it for aesthetic appeal or for practical reasons, e.g. the painting being framed has a wide unsightly margin, or a spacer is needed between glass and picture.

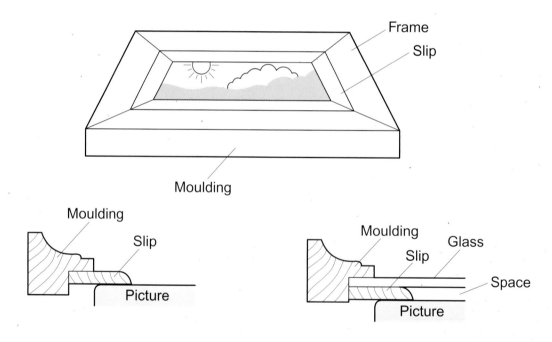

Slip frame

Oval frames

These mouldings are similar to swept frames in that they are produced in standard sizes in a variety of finishes. Making ovals is both costly and time-consuming. I find that a good supplier's catalogue with photos of their range of ovals is sufficient. The rare customer who wants an oval is usually happy to wait a few days. On the other hand, if you have a shop or workshop with good public access, I find it worthwhile to carry a range of swept frames and ovals – they can often inspire customers. However, you should only stock them once you have an established trade – it is best not to tie up money in slow-moving stock!

Box frames (shadow boxes/frames)

These are frames that contain either a three-dimensional object or require the subject to be set back from the glass. A box frame at its simplest is an outer frame with glass fitted in its rebate. A second frame (for this I use one of three ramin wood mouldings painted to the required colour with artists' acrylics) is then fitted into the rebate, holding the glass and giving a second rebate for the subject and backing.

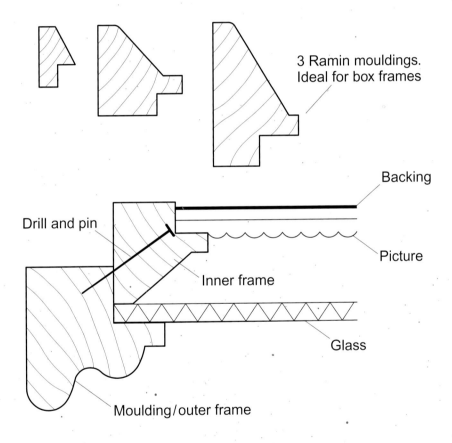

Box frame

You can achieve a similar effect using mount board. The visible mount is behind the glass, then several sheets of card, cut with a wider aperture than the first mount board, are fitted behind. Behind the sheets of card comes the picture. Thus there is a space between mount and picture.

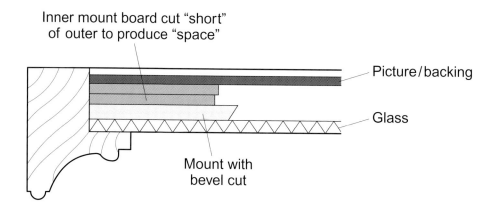

Creating 'space' using mount board

Double frames

Double frames are normally two sizes of the same moulding: the outer a decorated panel and the inner holding the subject. The easiest way to produce a double frame is to make the outer frame, then cut a piece of hardboard to fit. Next cut out the centre of the hardboard, allowing for a lip to fix the inner frame. This inner frame is then screwed to the hardboard, giving two frames with a hardboard surround which can also be decorated (but be sure to decorate the hardboard panel before fixing the frames!).

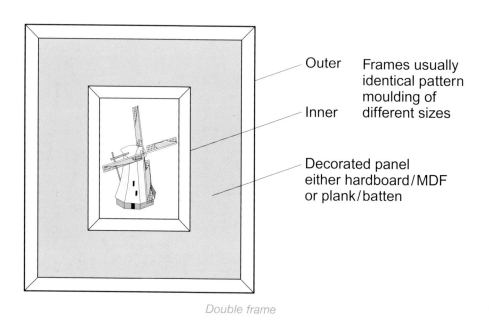

Double frame

I recently made a double frame for a hotel that had very striking wallpaper on vast walls. The prints they had chosen were large but still looked small on the wall; so we made double frames and decorated the hardboard surround with the same wallpaper, creating large and very striking pictures.

Mirror frames

Basically, mirrors are framed in the same way as any other panel-type subject. If you are framing mirrors to sell on spec, buy bevelled mirrors that will look very good in their frames. They should be hung with mirror plates to stop them getting knocked off the wall and also to keep them flat on the wall so that they can be easily looked into. There are also several designs of secret hangings for fixing mirror frames to walls.

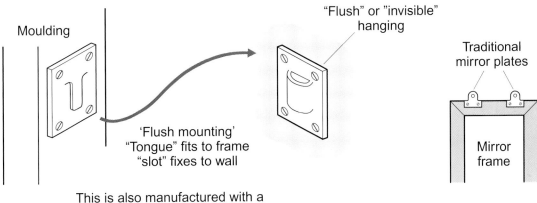

Moulding

"Flush" or "invisible" hanging

Traditional mirror plates

Mirror frame

'Flush mounting'
"Tongue" fits to frame
"slot" fixes to wall

This is also manufactured with a
locking device to prevent removal

There is one rule that you must follow when framing mirrors, and that is to blacken the rebate. If you look at the edge of a framed mirror you will often see the unsightly reflection of the back of the rebate. When framing mirrors, it is thus important after you have made the frame that you blacken the inside of the rebate with artists' black acrylic, or with felt-tip pen or stain.

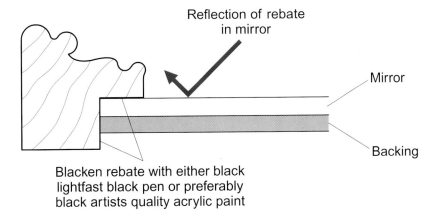

Reflection of rebate in mirror

Mirror

Backing

Blacken rebate with either black
lightfast black pen or preferably
black artists quality acrylic paint

Profiles

Moulding patterns are normally classified by the supplier according to their reference system. I always renumber them with my own system, i.e. AF/1, AF/2, to simplify my sample board – and to stop people from finding my sources of moulding too easily! However, it is worth knowing the names given to general styles of moulding.

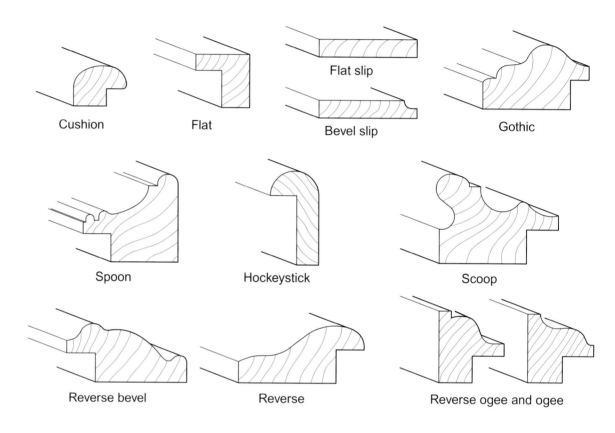

Cushion   Flat   Flat slip

Bevel slip   Gothic

Spoon   Hockeystick   Scoop

Reverse bevel   Reverse   Reverse ogee and ogee

Common moulding examples

Mounts, Matts and Mountboard

As I explained earlier, the mount is for decorative enhancement and separating the picture from the glass. There are literally hundreds of colours and textures of mount boards, giving you an endless range of combinations. The only limit is your imagination. One tip is not to overstate your mounts. Remember that you are complementing the subject, not dominating or completely overwhelming it. Interestingly, you will frequently get customers who want, for example, a red sunset framed in red to go with their red wallpaper or maroon carpet. My experience is that they have a picture they want framed; if you frame it with the aim of enhancing the picture, the end result will normally fit in with their decor, no matter how bizarre! You will, however, frequently get carpet samples, wallpaper and curtains, all to be matched to the framing!

Mounts fall into several categories:

Single mounts

The simplest, this is a single cut-out sheet to surround the picture.

Multiple mounts

The next type is the multiple mount, which is several sheets of different colours, or tones, or textures cut with an increasing aperture. The effect is of an outer colour with bands of varying colour receding towards the subject, giving an increased depth and leading the eye into the frame and its subject. You can have double, triple or multiple mounts, but remember the depth of your moulding rebate – it might need to be very deep! Also, there is no hard-and-fast rule as to the width of overlap. What looks best will vary from one picture to another.

Multiple mounts are held together using a single length of double-sided tape. Use your dividers to ensure accuracy.

Decorated mounts

The next category is the decorated mount. You will find an endless array of decorated tape banding pre-prepared in a variety of designs for you to apply to your mount. The traditional mount decoration is called 'wash line', which is basically a series of delicate lines drawn onto the matt with a delicate colour wash applied between two or several of the lines.

Washline mounts

To produce washline mounts, you will need:

a. a draughtsman's ruling pen
b. a straight-edge rule with a raised lip to keep the ruler and wet ink apart
c. a very fine pin
d. card offcuts to check your colours and the flow of pen and brush
e. a fine-pointed brush – size 3, 4 or 5
f. a sharp pencil
g. a pair of dividers.

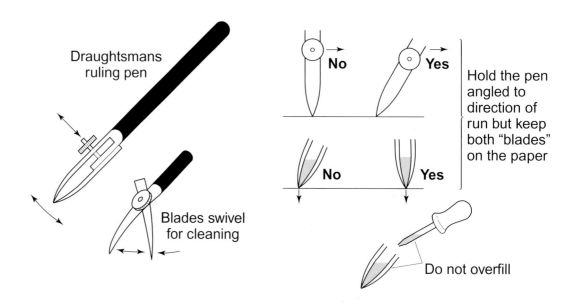

Draughtsmans
ruling pen

Blades swivel
for cleaning

No   Yes

No   Yes

Hold the pen
angled to
direction of
run but keep
both "blades"
on the paper

Do not overfill

Using a draughtsman's ruling pen

For drawing lines, I use coloured acrylic inks, which are fade-proof and which I water down to keep the lines subtle. A draughtsman's ruling pen (the pen usually found with sets of instruments) is a pair of pointed sprung blades that meet at the point and are adjusted by a knurled knob to set the width of line. You will need the de-luxe version with a movable lower blade to ensure you keep the pen clean. The pen is charged with a pipette or dropper that comes with the bottle of ink.

Deciding on the position of the lines is easy. For an even mount (the same width all round), reverse the mount board and place it on a card offcut. Then draw a line from the corner of the board to the corner of the aperture. Do this very accurately. Repeat for all four corners. Taking your dividers, open them along one of the mitre lines to the distance from the first washline will be to the edge of the aperture (if you have got locking or threaded dividers, all the better). With one point on the corner and the other where the first line is to go, mark the position of the line through the card with a pin to create a barely-visible hole on the face.

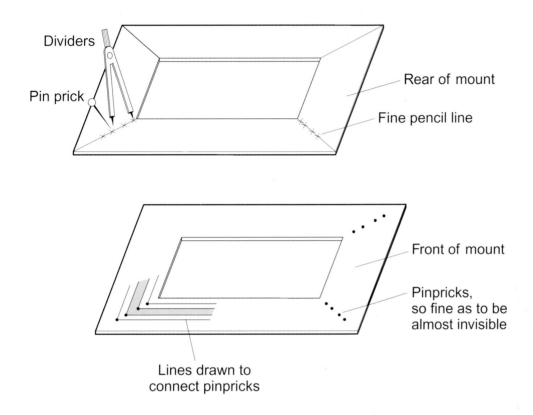

Dividers

Pin prick

Rear of mount

Fine pencil line

Front of mount

Pinpricks,
so fine as to be
almost invisible

Lines drawn to
connect pinpricks

Washline mounts

Repeat this on the other three corners, then readjust the point dividers to the next space you require. Place one point on the first mark then pierce the card and repeat on the other three sides. Repeat the process until you have all points marked out, then turn the mount board over and connect the dots (pin pricks) with your draughtsman's ruling pen. There is a small patent plastic insert that you can use to establish your points on the corner, but I still use my old method as I am then sure I will have a wash line that corresponds to the cut-out of the mount.

To draw the wash line, line up the straight edge with two adjacent pinholes. Then place the charged pen on the card against the straight edge and in one movement draw the line, holding the pen slightly off vertical while at the same time keeping both tips of the nib in contact with the card. Don't overload the pen with ink, or gravity will cause it to blob. Move positively and do not hesitate! Repeat on all four sides of the card and for as many lines as you think will complement the picture.

Having drawn the lines and allowed them to dry, apply a wash between two of the lines using a fine brush, usually a pointed brush (size 4). Start at a corner with a neat line following the mitre line, then in a careful continuous movement paint the colour between the lines around the mount (not over them, or your line will vary in colour intensity). Do not go back on yourself and don't stop until you can stop right against (and not over) your start point. Leave to dry.

WASHLINE MOUNT

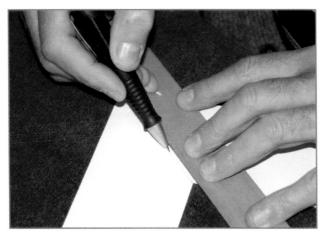

*1. Draw line from inner corner to outer corner
of mount, repeat for each corner.*

2. Shows diagonal lines on corners.

3 & 4. Use dividers to establish line positions.

*5. Use as fine a needle as possible to 'prick' mount board
to establish points of reference on face of mount.*

*6. Charge the lining pen (over a piece of scrap board).
Draw short 'test' line to ensure good flow.*

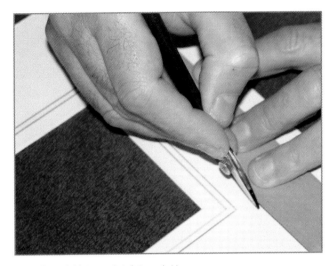

7 & 8. Carefully draw your lines from point (pin prick) to point (pin prick).

9. Carefully charge pen between EACH line.

10. Draw the final line and allow to dry.

11. The lines ready for their wash.

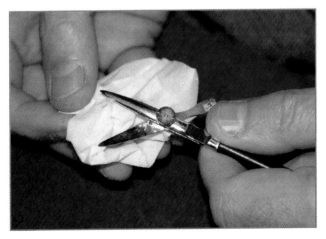

12. Open pen and clean thoroughly after use.

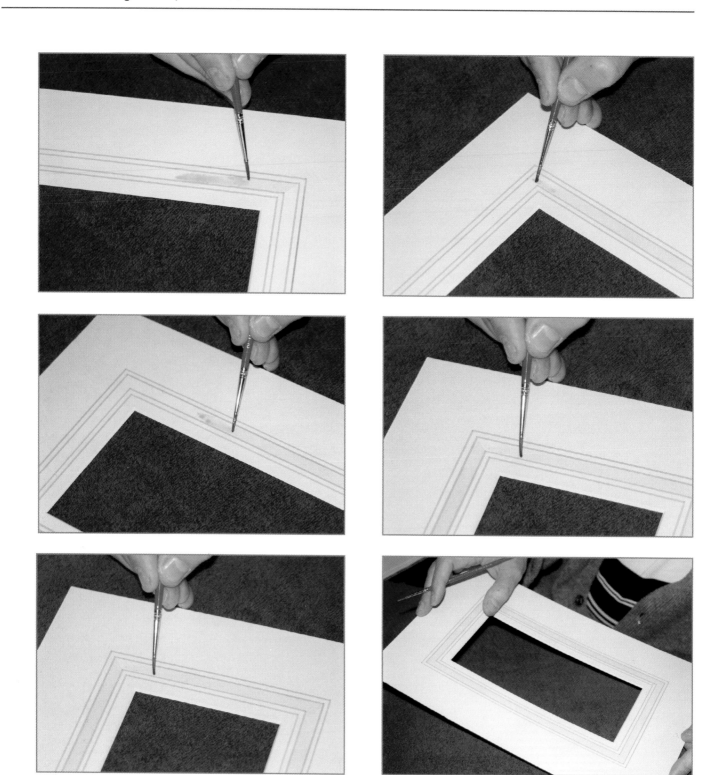

13, 14, 15, 16 & 17. Use the same coloured ink or watercolour greatly watered down for wash. Start in a corner,
working swiftly right around without going back on yourself until you return to the first corner. Bring the wash up
to this point <u>without</u> crossing the first wash –
great care and accuracy is the secret.

18. The washline mount.

The colour wash should be the same ink you use to draw the lines, only watered down until it's a thin tint of the original. You can, and I often do, use artists' watercolour (from an artist's sketch box with pans) to get the colour and effect I want. Practice will get you perfect wash lines – and here I stress they must be perfect. Nothing looks more amateurish than badly executed lining work. You can also combine your wash line with multiple mounts or gold lining using either pens or leaf. You will find yourself forever studying frames for ideas. Great sources of inspiration are very old frames round pictures brought in for reframing. The old framers achieved wonderful effects with very limited materials.

Oval mounts

Oval mounts are virtually impossible to cut without some kind of machine, be that a set of the big micrometre-thread oval cutters that cut both card and glass, or the simple arm on an offset base that describes an oval. This second device is your best solution until you want to splash out on a full-size cutting machine (the machine I possess has a fitting to take a drawing pen for producing oval wash lines – I've never tried to wash line an oval mount by hand!). Be very accurate when cutting your oval mount and assembling it into the frame, as inaccuracies will shout out at you!

Mount-cutting and mount preparation are probably the most time-consuming part of the frame-making process. I have a basic range of mount effects that I know I can execute quickly, neatly and effectively to ensure I do not become bogged down on any one frame. Time is money, so if a customer wants intricate and lavish work you should charge for it.

Three-Dimensional Objects, Box Frames and Display Cases

From time to time you will get 3D objects to frame, the most common being medals and coins. The coins are best framed in mount board individually cut to take them. I do this by placing the coin on the mount board, tracing it faintly in pencil and carefully cutting out the disc with a scalpel. There is a special cutter for this purpose, a compass-like device holding a blade which you rotate through the card. It works very well.

Medals are often mounted on velvet or silk glued onto a backing. The medals are then fixed on a bar. Once again, don't damage the ribbons when you frame medals. Give them an expansive frame. Close-framed, they look insignificant! The framing equipment you use is also ideal for making display cases of all descriptions. You will find that your local builders' merchant carries various wood mouldings for the carpentry trade. These you can adapt easily to framing or making display cases along with the various prepared timber lengths (but always use the best-quality kiln-dried timber). Your mitre guillotine will cut angles other than 45 degrees; in fact, it will cut any angle up to 90 degrees. Remember that if you make frames or cases that require any work with power tools, routers or saws, they create huge dust problems for your other framing activities: I would always recommend a separate 'dusty' work area or room.

As with all aspects of framing, the wholesalers now carry a range of box-framing devices, extensions to moulding, spacing bars. Use them by all means, but do not buy all sorts of patent aids when you start framing: they are a drain on resources and can be gradually added to your equipment as you find you have need of them.

Tapestries and Embroideries

Tapestries

The system I use for stretching tapestries I first devised 25 years ago, and it has never failed me. In recent years, I have seen tapestries I stretched and framed then, and they are still perfect. So I can say with certainty that the following method has withstood the test of time.

First measure the tapestry exactly then add 3 mm to each side length. Then make the stretch frame. This comprises a wood frame on a cardboard sheet. For the frame I carry ramin battens or planks in the following sizes: 40 x 5mm (1½ x ¼in.) for small, 50 x 5mm (2 x ¼in.) for medium, and 64 x 5mm (2½ x ¼ in.) for large tapestries. Cut your wood batten to the size you have measured – that's the outer side of the frame – glue and clamp the mitres, spread glue on one face of the wood frame (I use PVA wood glue) and place on top of an offcut sheet of mount board. Place the whole assembly under weights to dry overnight.

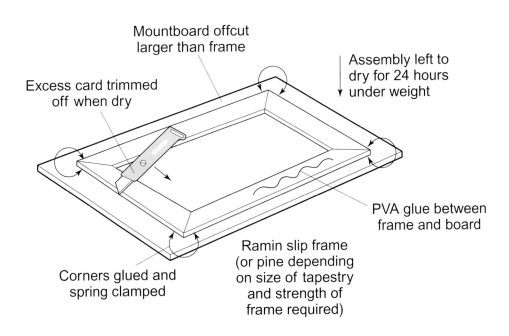

Tapestry stretcher frame

Once the frame is dry, trim the card to the frame edge with a Stanley knife then stretch on the tapestry. Simply start at one corner, hold and staple (using a stationery staple gun with 6mm staples – they are easier to remove if necessary than heavy duty DIY staples), making sure that the staples are in the wood, not the card.

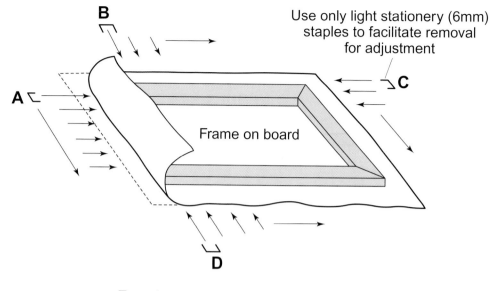

B

A

Frame on board

Use only light stationery (6mm)
staples to facilitate removal
for adjustment

C

D

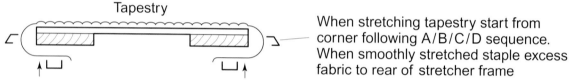

Tapestry

When stretching tapestry start from
corner following A/B/C/D sequence.
When smoothly stretched staple excess
fabric to rear of stretcher frame

Stretching tapestry

Work down the length and width, making sure you are dead straight and pulling the tapestry into position. Follow with the remaining two sides. Here you will have to pull much harder to align the tapestry. The more distorted the customer has made the tapestry, the bigger the battle! If the tapestry is very badly distorted, thicken the wood on the stretcher to take the strain. The result should be a perfectly flat tapestry, held with all the stitches straight. Again, practice makes perfect. I invariably box-frame my tapestries so that the fluffiness of the surface is not crushed by the glass. The inner frame I usually paint to match the predominant tapestry colour.

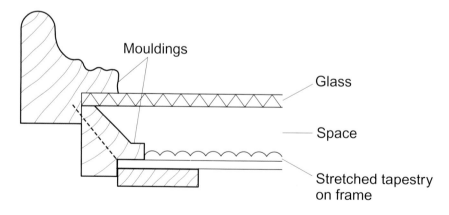

Mouldings

Glass

Space

Stretched tapestry
on frame

Box-framed tapestry

STRETCHING A TAPESTRY

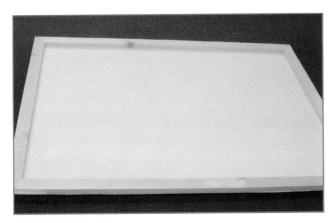

1. The frame, wood strip/batten is glued to mount board for extra strengh/ support.

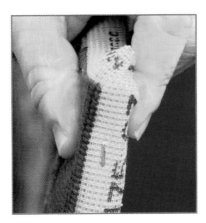

2. Fold edge around frame.

3 . Start stapling from corner.

4. Pull/fold round frame.

5. Staple (please note I am using heavy duty staples for photographic clarity).

6, 7, 8, 9, 10. Continue pulling, aligning and stapling along side until all edges are fixed and tapestry is flat, straight and taut.

7.

8.

9.

10.

11, 12, 13, 14, 15. Fold and staple the corners

13.

14.

15.

16. The stretched tapestry ready to be framed. .

There is only one potential problem with this method, and that is corrosion of the staples damaging the fabric. So as an added precaution I have always put a minute dab of copydex over the staples to keep them moisture-free. As a result, 25-year-old tapestries still have bright metal staples. Copydex is the only glue apart from resin 'W' wood adhesive (PVA) that I keep in the workshop. A latex-based glue, it is totally inert once cured. (Incidentally, if you are pruning trees, paint it on the cut ends to seal the wounds!)

Cross-stitch & needlepoint

For cross-stitch and needlepoint, I cut a thin white (acid-free) card and punch the edges of the card with a ring-binding punch, allowing plenty of space for the picture. The fixings are covered by the mount or slip. The needlepoint is then stitched onto the card.

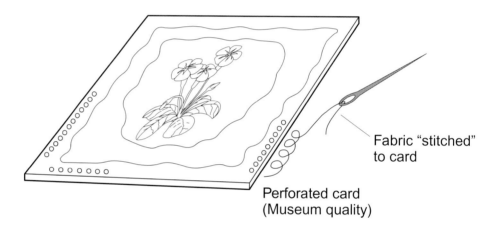

Fabric "stitched" to card

Perforated card (Museum quality)

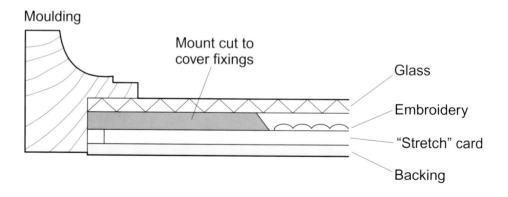

Moulding

Mount cut to cover fixings

Glass

Embroidery

"Stretch" card

Backing

Embroidery/cross-stitch

The second method is to take a card (acid-free) and put double-sided tape on the rear of the card and bring the fabric round to stick it on the rear, pulling the face taut. Once it is positioned and held, use masking tape to lock down the edges. If you use this method, go to the extreme edge of the fabric so that any damage the glues in the tapes inflict can be removed without detriment to the artwork. The third method is to 'lace' the cross stitch onto the card by folding the ends of the fabric round the card then lacing up the sides as per the sequence of photos on page 102.

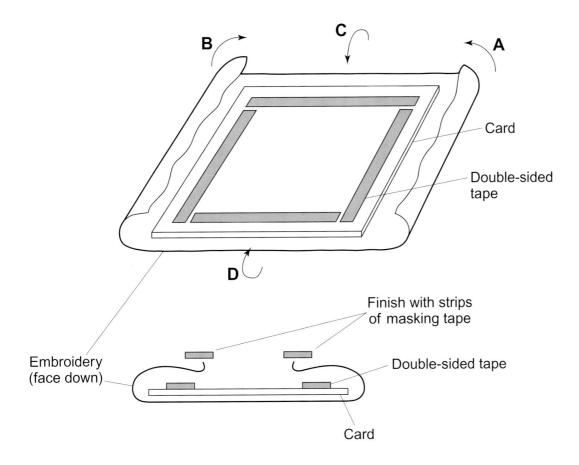

Card and double-sided tape

1 & 2. Measure artwork.

3 & 4. Cut backing board to size.

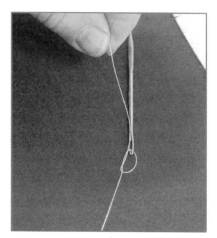 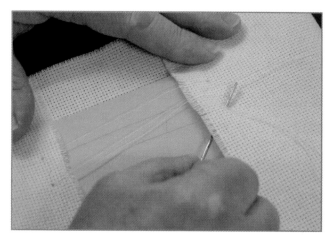

5. Knot cotton thread onto needle. Leave bobbin loose on floor or bench so you can pull the thread as you need it.

6, 7 & 8. Start at one end and 'bootlace' the thread through the fabric keeping straight and well in from edge.

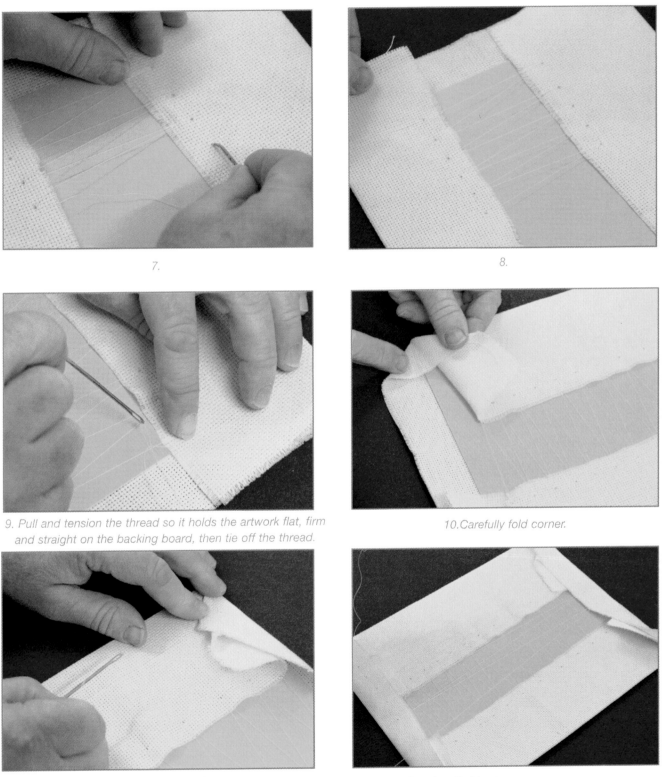

7.

8.

9. Pull and tension the thread so it holds the artwork flat, firm and straight on the backing board, then tie off the thread.

10. Carefully fold corner.

11, 12, 13. Repeat the bootlacing in opposite direction. Pull taut.

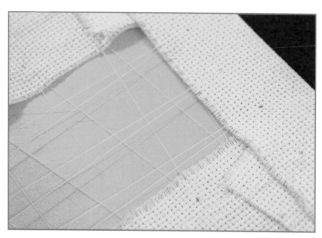

14. Detail showing lacing in both directions holding all four edges firmly.

15.

When you make a box frame using the battens, first cut the frame while at the same time cutting the battens. Make the frame up and, when dry, clean and fit the glass. Then fit the four battens to form the box. Pin and glue to the rear of the rebate. Having done this, cut four pieces of identical-width batten to fit to the outside of the box that is in the frame. It must be a snug, exact fit. Glue and clamp it to the outside of the box, and in doing so you will have formed a rebate to accommodate the backing board.

I once had a customer with a very special embroidery who wanted the work suspended in a frame with no fixings. My first reaction was 'How?', the second, 'Impossible'; but he insisted, so I asked him to go away and put two 'loops' (fold over and stitch the top and bottom) in the top and bottom of the piece, which he did. I then made a box frame using the 40mm (1½ in.) ramin battens with a turn-button back. I drilled through the sides of the box and inserted two 12mm (½ in.) pieces of dowel. The fabric was then hung top and bottom on the dowel and the back closed and taped.

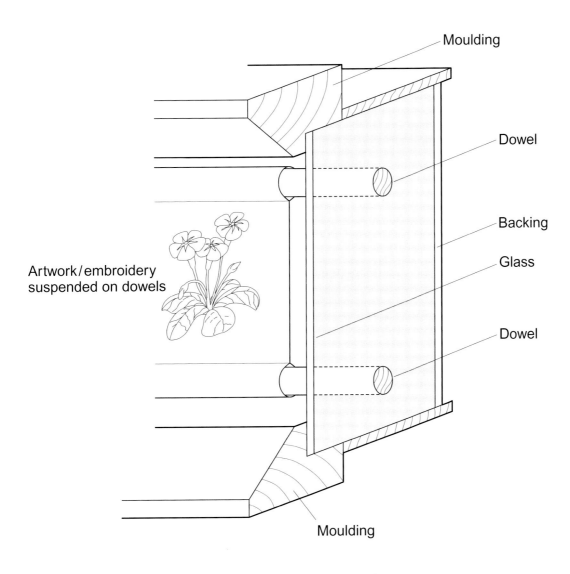

Moulding

Dowel

Backing

Glass

Dowel

Artwork/embroidery
suspended on dowels

Moulding

Box frame with suspended artwork

When I first knew my wife, I bought her some very expensive, exquisite lace handkerchiefs while I was on the Continent. Unbeknown to me, she had them framed. I did not think any more of this until we moved house. I was packing the framed lace when I noticed a yellow stain on each of the handkerchiefs. I took the frame to the workshop and opened it up to discover that the framer had stuck the handkerchiefs down with some sort of glue or double-sided tape that had rapidly attacked the cloth, leaving brittle yellow patches. Needless to say the lace work was ruined, with the result that a treasured sentimental item had to be thrown away. The handkerchiefs should have been mounted with very fine stitches of matching cotton sewn onto white museum board. If you use glues, beware! Think about how to mount artwork with its long-term welfare in mind. You are the expert; the customer trusts you and thus you have a responsibility to them.

Looking through various suppliers' catalogues, you will see that there are numerous needlework stretching and mounting devices. Try them out until you find the system that suits you best.

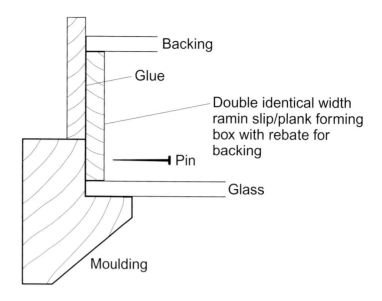

Forming a rebate to accommodate the backing board

Stretching Canvas

You will either come across artists who want their canvas stretched, or, more commonly, a customer who has bought a painting on canvas which has been rolled for transport and needs to be remounted on a stretcher frame. Stretcher frames are sold in prefabricated lengths. They can be obtained from wholesalers and also from art shops. The ends have a 'tongue and slot' configuration that allows for a pair of wooden wedges per corner once the canvas is stretched onto the frame. The canvas can be tensioned by tapping in the wedges to expand the corner joint.

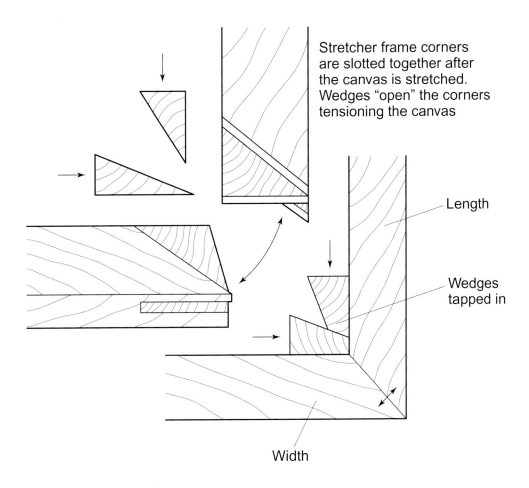

Stretcher frame corners are slotted together after the canvas is stretched. Wedges "open" the corners tensioning the canvas

Length

Wedges tapped in

Width

Stretcher-frame corners slotted together

To stretch a canvas, firstly fit the four sides of the stretcher frame together and place on a bench. Using your set square, check that the frame is square (if it is not square, you will have problems when it comes to the framing). Lay the canvas face down on the bench and place the stretcher frame on top. If it is a picture you are mounting, make sure you align the holes from its previous fixing to correspond to where you will be fixing the stretcher frame sides. Once you are satisfied the canvas is accurately fixed, take the centre of the first edge (usually the one facing you), fold the canvas up the side of the stretcher bar and pin either using the traditional tack, or, as I do, a 6mm stationery gun stapler. Then take the *opposite* bar, pull the canvas taut over the edge using a pair of canvas pliers (or your hands, depending on your grip), and staple. Repeat this procedure on the other two sides.

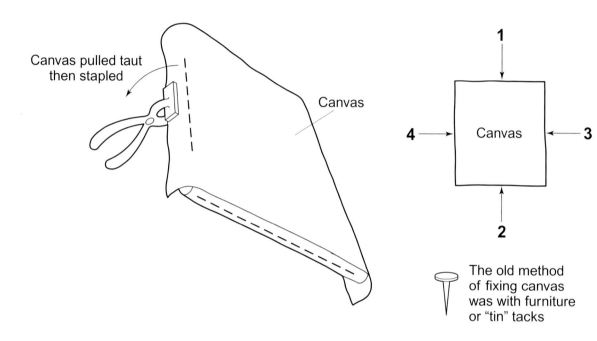

Canvas pulled taut then stapled

Canvas

1

4   Canvas   3

2

The old method of fixing canvas was with furniture or "tin" tacks

Pulling canvas taut and stapling

You will now have the canvas held on the stretcher at four points, one on each side. Start on one side and from the middle to the corner stretch and staple the canvas until the entire side is stapled. Repeat this on the opposite side, pulling the canvas taut. Then repeat on the other two sides.

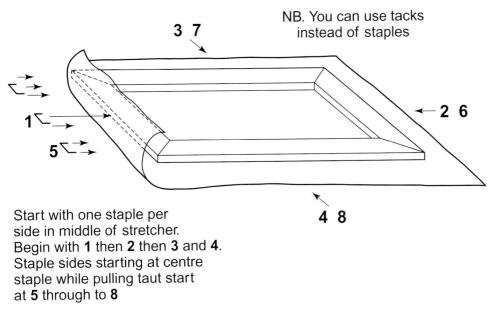

NB. You can use tacks
instead of staples

3 7

1

5

2 6

4 8

Start with one staple per
side in middle of stretcher.
Begin with **1** then **2** then **3** and **4**.
Staple sides starting at centre
staple while pulling taut start
at **5** through to **8**

Stapling or tacking

Once the canvas is stretched over the frame, lay it face down and fold the corners one at a time. Pull the canvas over the back of the frame and hold it down. Then take the two side flaps, pull these up, hold them down and staple both to the back of the stretcher frame. Repeat on the other corners, then staple the canvas all round onto the back of the stretcher frame. Once it is neatly fixed, insert the eight wedges and gently tap them in to tension the canvas – it should be smooth and taut, but not overstretched to distortion. (NB: when stretching tapestries you start at the corner of each side, whereas with a canvas you start in the middle.)

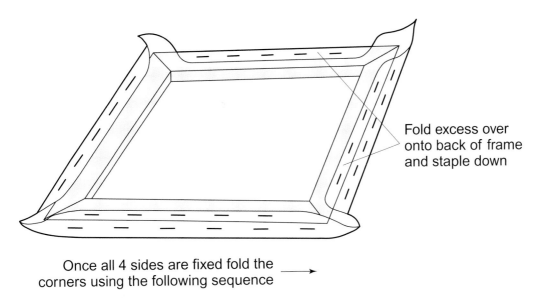

Fold excess over
onto back of frame
and staple down

Once all 4 sides are fixed fold the
corners using the following sequence

Fold and staple excess

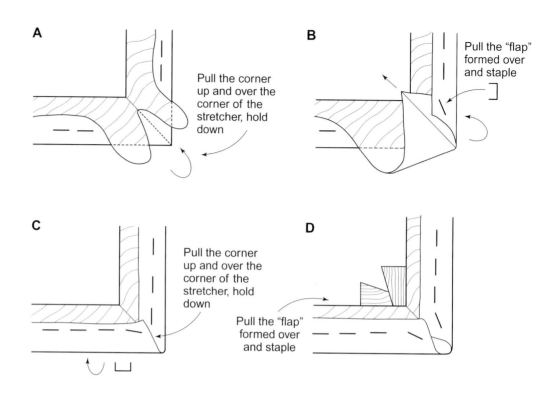

A

Pull the corner up and over the corner of the stretcher, hold down

B

Pull the "flap" formed over and staple

C

Pull the corner up and over the corner of the stretcher, hold down

D

Pull the "flap" formed over and staple

A+B, C+D corners fold and staple

Once again, get some canvas, some stretcher frames and practise; it's best not to use someone's precious picture to train yourself on. Once you have perfected the technique and can produce professional stretched canvases, you can sell them to your artist customers with no risk of waste.

STRETCHING A CANVAS

1. Using a pair of canvas stretching pliers, pull taught and tap in tacks. Start from the middle and work to the corners

2. This is a painting being re-stretched – use the original holes where possible to maintain integrity of canvas.

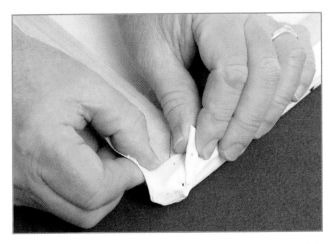

3 & 4. Fold corners carefully.

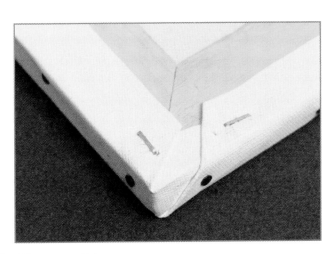

5 & 6. Staple the back of the canvas flat.

 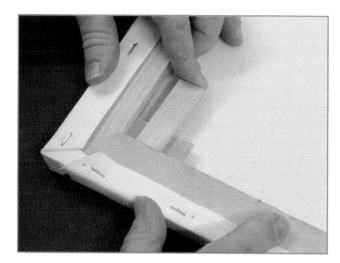

7, 8, 9,10. Tap in wedges – work on opposite sides and be careful not to <u>over</u> stretch.

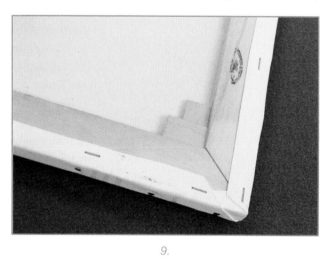

9.

10.

11. The wedged and stretched canvas.

Stretching Watercolours

Some customers will request that their watercolours be stretched. You will see many artists stretch their paper onto a board before painting. In this method the back of the paper is moistened (though not soaked), then taped to a backing board using gum-strip tape (never synthetic tape), and the whole allowed to dry. The paper expands upon wetting and then shrink-dries, the tape holding the paper and making it taut. This method is normally used when framing a badly cockled watercolour.

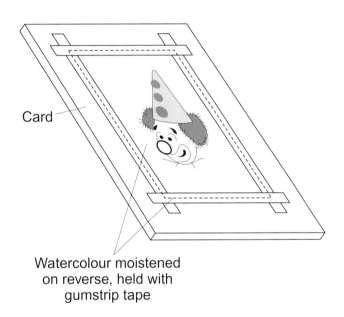

Card

Watercolour moistened
on reverse, held with
gumstrip tape

Stretching a watercolour.

STRETCHING A WATERCOLOUR

1. Watercolour to be stretched on its acid free backing board (trimmed to size).

2, 3 & 4. Cut strips of gum tape for all four sides.

3.

4.

5. Moisten the reverse of the watercolour (DO NOT OVERWET!).

6. Wet the four lengths of tape.

 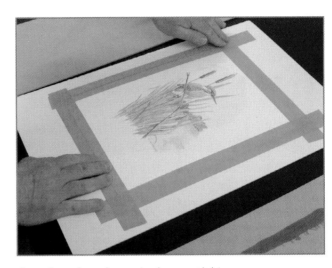

7 & 8. *Lay the picture on the backing and tape along the edges. Leave to dry overnight.*

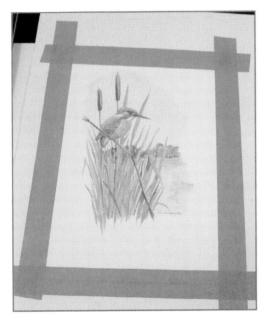

9. *The stretched, smooth watercolour.*

Drumming

Drumming is the stretching of a picture executed on sheepskin or calfskin vellum. Like stretching watercolours, it entails moistening the rear of the vellum then folding and taping the edges over a wood panel and allowing to dry. Once again, be very careful not to split the vellum, or to over-tension and bend or break the backing board. This is a process now so rare that you might never need it, but it is worth knowing what to do!

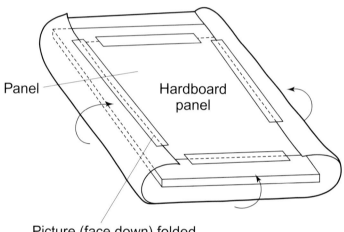

Panel

Hardboard panel

Picture (face down) folded over edge of board and taped to the board using gumstrip paper tape

'Drumming' - stretching a sheepskin vellum

Dry Mounting

Many framers now use dry mounting, which is basically the sticking down of a picture using a sheet of resin glue that is heated to become adhesive, thus bonding the picture to the backing. You often see photographs on framed canvas, like an oil painting. These are dry mounted. To get the picture flat requires a vacuum press, a glass-top box from which the air is extracted. The vacuum pulls the picture, resin and backing together perfectly flat and the press heats the resin at the same time, causing it to bond the whole into a sandwich. This process also bonds a clear plastic covering film on top of the picture.

I have never used dry mounting and have never had a demand for it. The suppliers on the other hand supply pre-glued cold mounting board, where the glue is covered by a film of wax paper. It works very well for sticking pictures down flat.

To prevent air bubbles, use as follows:

Cut the board slightly larger than the picture and place on the bench. From the bottom edge of the board, lift up and peel back about 4cm (1½in.) of the covering paper and fold down flat. Carefully align and stick the bottom edge of the picture to the exposed board. Then, with one hand between the board and the picture, grip the cover paper; with the other hand, using a *clean* lino-printing roller, peel the cover paper while at the same time rolling the picture flat. Keep going until you reach the top edge. This method should stick the picture down without air bubbles. Trim the board down to size.

Once again practise on old prints and paper before attempting the operation on a customer's picture. A good tip should you get an air bubble is to flatten it by pricking the picture with a fine pin and rolling down flat, allowing the air to escape. With care this can be done invisibly, but of course it is much better not to get air bubbles in the first place.

Kraft-Paper Backing

On the theme of stretching, in some parts of the world it is fashionable to cover the back of the frame with kraft paper. To do this, cut a piece of kraft paper to fit loosely over the backing board. Moisten the back and stick on with gum-strip tape. When dry, the kraft paper held to the frame by the gum strip will stretch to give a drumskin-taut backing. You can also glue a sheet of kraft paper directly to the moulding but using gumstrip is faster and easier!

Gum-Strip Taping

To prevent the ingress of dust or insects into the frame via the fine crack between moulding rebate and glass, you should tape the inside of the rebate and the glass with gum-strip tape.

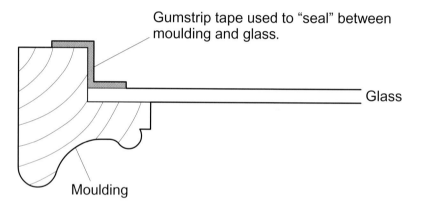

Gumstrip tape used to "seal" between moulding and glass.

Glass

Moulding

Gum-strip taping

Fire Screens

Fire screens are in effect a picture frame with a top handle and a pair of feet screwed on. I have seen various designs of fire screen fittings at framing wholesalers, but the best I have found have come from sundries wholesalers. These are firms that supply the cabinet-making and carpentry trades. The firm I have always used is called Frank B. Scraggs.

One of the differences between a fire screen and a hanging frame is the back finishing. You do not tape up the rear, but rather put the hardboard or MDF back panel in place and cover the moulding or backing joint with a wood strip or thin plank.

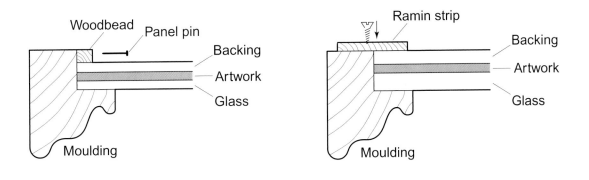

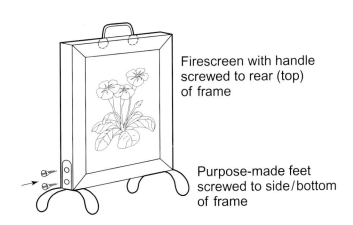

Finishing the back of a fire screen

Box frames make good fire screens, holding artificial flower arrangements, plates, small carpets, tapestries – the scope is endless.

Gilding

Gilding is the process whereby a surface is covered in some form of metallic leaf. It is called leaf because it comes in very fine sheet form, usually in a book to separate the individual sheets. This includes gold leaf, which usually comes in books of 25 sheets approximately 80 x 80 mm square and .001 mm thick – so fine in fact that it crumples or blows away in the slightest draught.

It is picked up using what is known as a 'gilder's tip'. This in effect is a fine flat brush made of badger hair. Brush your face with this to pick up some skin oil or static, to help the leaf stick, and transfer it to a gilder's pad or cushion – a pad made with fine animal skin (calf or pig). The leaf is cut to size using a gilder's knife, then placed onto the workpiece and tamped into place using fine soft-hair (usually sable) brushes or mops. Then agate burnishers are used to rub the leaf to produce a high shine. Small pieces of leaf can be applied using your finger. Once again, wipe your finger down the outside(!) of your nose to grease it before picking up the precut fragment and placing it where you want it.

Aside from the leaf in book form mentioned above, there exists a variety of gold leaf that is pressed into the surface of fine paper, making handling much easier. It is applied in a similar way to plastic picture transfers. Apart from gold leaf there are also imitation gold and silver leafs made of metal alloys, which are produced in larger, sheet form and are somewhat easier to apply. However, these will tarnish if not protected. Such protection used to be achieved by coating the leaf with shellac or wax, but now, more often than not, acrylic varnish is used. Lastly, there are the gilt paints and creams or wax pastes. These are mainly used for making good your moulding spine, i.e. where the pinholes or clamp marks are visible. Gold paint and waxes do not produce the sort of finish effects you get on professional frames.

Preparing your surface for gilding

If it is an old frame, and you intend to gild it completely, clean off the old gilt. For this, I use 20 grams of bicarbonate of soda with the same amount of detergent in I litre of water. Stir well and rub onto the surface with a piece of sponge. Then rub with a toothbrush to remove any stubborn gilt. Wipe off and rinse with methylated spirits then rub smooth. Fine wire wool formed round a stick, like a cotton bud, is useful. Having cleaned your frame, make sure it is in good condition. Fill in holes, cracks, chips, etc. As with making good new frames, I use Brummer's Interior Stopping for this task – I have yet to find anything as good!

For gilding you will then have to apply gesso. (Please note that the polymer-based product used on artists' canvases and called 'gesso' is not the same product.) Apply the gesso in thin coats and, when dry, smooth it with a very fine sandpaper. This is repeated for up to 12 coats. The gesso can also be tinted with dry pigment – this is usually dark burnt sienna. The prepared surface is then coated in size. Usually called 'bole', size is a fine clay, usually coloured red. Several coats are applied. Allow to dry and, using the finest abrasive and very gentle pressure, smooth – but do not rub through – the red coats.

Mix up a gilder's liquor – I use a teacup into which I put seven parts distilled water with three parts methylated spirits. Mix well then paint this onto the surface and wait until it has become tacky. (Place a knuckle of a bent finger onto the surface and lift it away. If it releases with a 'click', the surface is ready for the leaf.) Once the frame has been gilded, do not touch it for 12 hours, then polish gently with a piece of cotton wool (or if you wish to burnish, wait 6 hours before burnishing the gold-leaf surface with an agate burnisher). Work slowly and thoroughly.

A few hints on gilding

1. Do not wear clothes that carry a static charge.
2. To reduce the sheet size of your leaf, take three or four leaves between their tissues and tear into quarters. Do not cut as you will damage or crimp the edges. These quarters can be used in small areas.
3. Let your sheets overlap by 2–3mm and let them down gently onto the size, but do not let your fingers, or the gilder's tip, touch the size.
4. Do not attempt to get gold leaf into inaccessible areas. These are normally painted later with liquid gilt.
5. Varnish is not necessary over gold leaf unless it is to age the frame.

Gilding is a difficult, time-consuming process that is very expensive and takes a lot of practice to perfect. I have never found a commercial demand for it in a normal day-to-day picture-framing business, but it is worth looking at as your business grows and you look for more directions to expand in.

I left gilding well alone for a long time. It was only when I had a successful picture-framing business that I diversified into the more specialised services. Incidentally, bookbinding is a craft that fits in with framing if you have the space – but that's another story!

Picture Restoration

This is a side of framing I have always avoided. Many framers do picture restoration and in my experience pictures are more often ruined than they are enhanced unless the work is carried out by a professional. Picture restoration is a completely separate profession that requires training, experience and great skill. Your local museum or council gallery (or failing that, one of the major city museums) will probably furnish you with a list of restorers. I got the name of a restorer from an art auctioneers' and always refer restoration to that source.

If you really want to go into restoration, study the skill and if necessary take lessons – do it properly! Picture-frame restoration is an easier option. If you can master gilding, frame restoration will seem fairly straightforward; but bear in mind that where you are dealing with the mass-produced moulding of the last 50 years, it is probably easier to make a new frame. Old wood frames can be cleaned and repolished (remember that some may have been distressed and antiquated on purpose), and basic frame damage – involving chips, scratches and sprung mitres – is fairly easy to repair. The mitres can be easily rejoined, and scratches and chips can be filled and colour-matched or camouflaged - see the section on making good in Professional/Semi-professional Framing.

A customer of mine once brought me some beautiful old prints in rosewood frames that he had found in an attic. The glass was scratched and beyond repair, so I replaced it, cut new museum-quality mounts and backing, and lightly boot-polished the frames. The end result was stunning and much appreciated.

Using Offcuts

Whenever I have a quantity of assorted offcuts of moulding, glass, mount board, etc., I make up small frames (miniatures) that will take postcards, greetings cards and illustrations (a good way of recycling Christmas/birthday cards). Displayed in my workshop, these little pictures always sell as fast as I can produce them, effectively turning waste into profit. You can also use them with mirror offcuts to make small mirrors, which again are always popular. You can add mount board offcuts to the same small frames. Another idea is to make up and display assorted mounts at a cut price for local artists.

Glass remnants that are unusable can (and should) be taken to the local glass recycling centre. They now sell gadgets that break up your glass waste into fine waste, but I still prefer to recycle mine.

CONCLUSION

Uniquely, picture framing is an Art, a Craft and a Trade. It is a service to a community and, like plumbers and electricians, good picture framers will always be in demand.

Picture framing itself is a lucrative and immensely satisfying occupation that combines the technical, mechanical and artistic side of a person's nature. It is easy to start as it does not require permits or licences and for this picture framer it has produced many years of interest and satisfaction – I have seen the most incredible artwork and pictures, met interesting people and had the intense pleasure of being my own boss.

Even on a 'hobby' basis, to be able to frame pictures or other objects yourself, or as an artist, your own work, to a standard and presentation of your choice can greatly enhance the satisfaction of ownership or creation.

In this book I have tried to give you all the hints, tips and knowledge I have learned over the last 30 years of picture framing and whether you are interested in just framing your own work or in having a hobby that can also earn its keep or whether you wish to become a full time professional framer,

I sincerely hope you find it useful.

Happy Framing!

GLOSSARY

Bradawl	sharp spiked tool to start holes for screws
Box frame	a frame made for a 3 dimensional object, almost a hanging display case
Countersink	to set a screw or pin below the surface of the moulding
Calibration	measurements
Cockling	uneven undulations in paper caused by moisture
Distressed	made to look old/used
De-edge	make glass safer by blunting the cut edges
Foamcore	layered backing board with foam centre
Guillotine	fixed knife blade/s for cutting wood/card/paper
Gesso	layer acting as base on wood or canvas for paint/decoration
Hardware	various fittings of a picture frame, the fixings and hangings
Hardboard	backing board made from highly compressed sawdust
Jig	device to aid accurate drilling/cutting
Moulding/Molding	shaped ornamental edging, in this case to make up the picture frame
Mitre	the pair of 45-degree cuts which make a right angle when joined
Mitre block	the guide used when hand cutting moulding to 45-degrees mitres
Mount	to fix to a backing or a card surround, in framing, the coloured or plain card which surrounds the artwork between artwork and moulding
Matt	American term for 'mount'
Mountboard/Matt board	coloured, decorative, specially-made cardboard placed around the picture being framed
Mounts/Matts	*Double:* Ornamental card surrounding picture with a second slightly visible mount/matt underneath to deepen the mount effect and provide a strip of another colour or texture *Triple:* As above but three layers of card/mountboard *Washline:* Decoration on the mount using coloured ink lines and fine wash *French:* American term for washline mounts
Mount/Matt cutter	machine designed to cut mounts with a beveled cut
MDF Board	medium density fibreboard – a wood fibre board commonly used in 2mm thickness as picture frame backing
Mirror Plates	brass plates on back of framed mirrors to enable mirror to hang flat to wall

Panel Pins	small nails of varying lengths originally designed for fixing panels
Rebate	the recess in a picture frame (moulding) which takes the glass/backing and artwork
Rabbit	the old term for a rebate
Screw eyes/rings	screw-in fixings used to hang a picture frame
Stretcher	frame to support/hold tapestry/canvas
Soft Board	Soft wood fibre board used for insulation in building trade, also called insulation board
Sundries	the host of fittings and accessories available to picture framers
String Clamp	wire- or string-held set of clamps to dry a glued frame under pressure
Shadow Box	same as box frame – a frame with depth for a 3D effect or 3-dimensional artwork
Tenon Saw	small carpenter's saw used for fine work – originally used with mitre block to hand-cut moulding
Woodworm	beetle larvae that burrow in wood causing immense damage

LIST OF SUPPLIERS

UNITED KINGDOM

EUROMOULDINGS
21 Timberlaine Trading Estate
Decoy Road
Worthing
West Sussex BN14 8JH
Tel: 01903 205 825
Fax: 01903 206 666
info@euro-mouldings.co.uk

Unit 7 Tun Yard
Peardon Street
London SW8 3BW
Tel: 020 7498 2760

Mersey House
Heaton Mersey Industrial Estate
Heaton Mersey
Manchester SK4 3EA
Tel: 0161 432 7156

ASHWORTH and THOMPSON
Freeston Drive
Bulwell
Nottingham NG6 8UZ
Tel: 0115 927 8504
sales@ashworthandthompson.co.uk
www.ashworthandthompson.co.uk

LION
148 Garrison Street
Heartlands
Birmingham B9 4BN
Tel: 0121 773 1230
Fax: 0121 771 2540
info@lionpic.co.uk
www.lionpic.co.uk

LION SOUTH
Unit 3
Squirrels Trading Estate
Viveash Close
Hayes
Middlesex UB3 4RZ
Tel: 020 8848 4558
Fax: 020 8813 6241
south@lionpic.co.uk
www.lionpic.co.uk

D & J SIMONS & SONS Ltd.
122-150 Hackney Road
London E2 7QS
Tel: 020 7739 3744
Fax: 020 7739 4452
dsimons@djsimons.co.uk
www.djsimons.co.uk

FRANK B SCRAGG (sundries)
68 Vittoria Street
Birmingham B1 3PB
Tel: 0121 236 7219

REPUBLIC OF IRELAND

SISSLINGS MOULDINGS
Unit T1
Stillorgan Park Industrial Estate
Stillorgan
Co. Dublin
Ireland
Tel: +353 1 295 4131
Fax: +353 1 295 4978
www.sisslings.com

DENMARK

KIG IND
Nystedvej 3
DK-7400 HERNING
Denmark
Tel: +45 9 721 5545

INDIA

LION INDIA
Bird Jute Mill Compound,
200 Dakshinadri Road,
Kolkata 700048
India
Tel: +91 33 521 8162
Fax: +91 33 521 7551
lion@cal2.vsnl.net.in
www.lionindia.net

Depots in New Delhi
(lionpicture@bol.net.in) and Mumbai.

USA

FRAMING SUPPLIES
1237 Shipp Street
Hendersonville
NC 28791
Tel: 800 334 9060
info@framingsupplies.com
www.framingsupplies.com

SOUTH AFRICA

SUPREME MOULDINGS
1008 Katrol Ave
Robertville ext 10
1708 Roodepoort
Tel: 011 472 0870
www.suprememouldings.co.za

EXQUISITE MOULDINGS
7 Stellar Ave
Crown Mines ext 4
Johannesburg 2092
Tel: 011 839 1911
info@artmouldings.co.za
www.artmouldings.co.za

LANCO WOOD PRODUCTS
Industrial Ring Road
Parow 7490
Western Cape
Tel: 021 931 8127

CHINA

XIAMEN J'D WOODEN CRAFTS CO.
Liuying Hongtang Village
Tong Fu Town
Xinglin Xiamen
China 361027
Tel: +86 592 631 0001
Fax: +86 592 631 2699
www.junde.com

QUANZHOU LIYUAN CRAFT CO.
Xijin Industrial Area
Shuitou
Nan'an City
Fujian Province
China 362342
Tel: +86 595 8698 9092
Fax: +86 595 869 1093
www.liyuan-crafts.com

AUSTRALIA

M and N SUPPLIES LTD
24 Alex Avenue
Moorabbin
VIC 3189
Tel: +61 3 9553 5888
Fax: +61 3 9553 5999
National Tollfree:
1800 35 80 40
mail@mnsupplies.com.au
www.mnsupplies.com.au

ALL STATES FRAMING
45 Geddes Street
Mulgrave
VIC 3170
Tel: +61 3 9561 7533
Fax: +61 3 9560 8764
sales@allstatesframes.com.au

ALBION GLASS AND MIRROR CO.
Cnr Sandgate Rd and Gore Street,
Albion
Brisbane
Q 4010
Tel: +61 7 3262 6227
Fax: +61 7 3262 7605
National Tollfree:
1800 35 39 48
help@albionglass.com.au
www.albionglass.com.au

CHAMPTON PTY LTD.
145-147 Glenlyon Rd
Brunswick East
VIC 3057
Tel: +61 3 9387 0444

TEMPO ART PRODUCTS
Unit 2 Natalie Way
Balcatta
WA 6021
Tel: +61 8 9344 7222

INDEX